WARWICKSHIRE
BREWERIES

How to serve
and enjoy

FLOWERS BEERS

WARWICKSHIRE
BREWERIES

JOSEPH McKENNA

TEMPUS

Frontispiece: An advertisement for Flowers Beers.

First published 2006

Tempus Publishing Limited
The Mill, Brimscombe Port,
Stroud, Gloucestershire, GL5 2QG
www.tempus-publishing.com

British Library Cataloguing in Publication Data.
A catalogue record for this book is available from the British Library.

ISBN 0 7524 3755 0

Typesetting and origination by Tempus Publishing Limited.
Printed in Great Britain.

CONTENTS

ACKNOWLEDGEMENTS

My thanks to the staff of the Warwick, Stratford and Coventry Record Offices. My thanks also to Coventry Local Studies Library and Mrs Mary Warwood of Studley. Thanks are due again to Paul Taylor and Andy 'Bruce' Willis of the Local Studies Library, Birmingham, for scanning many of the illustrations, and Chris Ash for taking photographs.

INTRODUCTION

Beer (the assurance that God loves us) was first produced in England, in any real quantity, in the religious houses that catered for travellers and pilgrims. Many ancient inns, when attached to monastic houses, bore religious names such as the Angel, the Lamb & Flag and the Cross Keys, names that we are familiar with today, though may not be aware of their historical and religious significance. In pre-Reformation times, with no less than ninety-five days kept as religious holidays, there was no shortage of Church Ales, Whitsun Ales, Clerk Ales, Bride Ales, Help Ales (the money from which was given to the poor), all brewed by, or under the auspices of, the Church. It was the monasteries that became the great innovators, giving us the basis of the beer that we know today in all its many forms. It was the religious houses in the sixteenth century, with connections to the Continent, that introduced hops to counter the 'biscuity' sweetness of malted cereals. The hop added a bitterness to the beer, and gave it a pleasing aroma. English brewers at the time were using a variety of plants and herbs, including rosemary, bog myrtle and yarrow.

In the post-Reformation period the 'olde English inn' beloved of Dickensian stories came into being. It fulfilled the same function for travellers as the religious houses, providing a bed for the night, food and drink. At a time when the purity of drinking water could not be guaranteed, beer, brewed on the premises, was drunk as an alternative. Small beer, a very weak beer, was drunk by everybody, even children. William Shakespeare, a Warwickshire man, immortalised the late medieval inn in *The Taming of the Shrew*. He took the inn in his mother's village, Wilmcote, and gave us an intimate and amusing description of it and 'Marian Hacket, the fat Ale-wife of Wincot'. We learn of the Court Leet and the laws appertaining to brewing, laws enforced by Ale Conners, who tested for quality and quantity:

And say you would present her at the leet,
Because she brought stone jugs and no seal'd quarts.

This is a reference to serving beer in a jug without a pint measure, thus offering the chance of giving short measure – which was very much frowned upon then, and no less so today. Apart from testing that a full pint was given, the Conners also tested to see whether the beer had been adulterated. The usual custom was that an Ale Connor entered a house unannounced and called for a half-pint of beer. This he then poured on a wooden seat and, in his leather breeches, sat down on the spillage. Here he remained for half an hour. He could take a drink, smoke a pipe, but could not move. After half an hour, he rose. If he did so without the breeches sticking to the seat, the beer was pronounced wholesome. If he remained stuck then he knew sugar had been added to the brew, so that the house and its brewer were taken up before the Court Leet and fined. This activity is still continued to this day in Warwickshire, at Henley-in-Arden, though it is more in pageantry than enforcement. Today we have Trading Standards to deal with the rogues.

Commercial brewing within the county began at Birmingham in 1752. In the rest of the county, which is the area dealt with in this book, Coventry was the next town to establish what is known as a Common Brewery. William Summerfield and David Lloyd began brewing in Leicester Row in 1801. During the 1830s three major breweries were established within the county. Of these, perhaps the most famous is that of Flowers of Stratford-upon-Avon. Perhaps not so well known is the Warwick & Leamington Brewery Co. of Saltisford, Warwick. Even so, its records have survived and we can see how it fared, how the company struggled, how they costed out the production of one brew of 30 barrels of beer at 1s 4d a gallon. There were hard times, competition was fierce, big fish swallowed up smaller fish, outsiders stepped in and breweries disappeared. Throughout these takeovers, one brewery emerged supreme in Warwickshire – Flowers. It had been ruthless too, seeing off the competition, even going to court on one occasion to preserve its good name. But it too disappeared in all but name, its brewery closed down and production moved elsewhere.

Throughout this time, as the big breweries battled it out, in towns and villages across the county small breweries continued as they had always done. Home-brew houses we should correctly call them, brewing for themselves and possibly supplying beer for christenings, weddings and funerals. It was small-scale stuff, with the brewers scraping a living. By the 1890s the 'big boys' began to look with envious eyes upon them. This was the start of the tied-house system. Pubs across the county, indeed across the country, were snapped up so the big breweries could sell even more of their beer. And they all went, every one, taken over by the bigger breweries. The last home-brew house to be taken over was in an obscure part of the county called Warings Green. The Blue Bell ceased brewing in 1968. Ignominy of ignominies, it was taken over by a cider maker, Bulmer's of Hereford.

During the 1970s and '80s brewing was in turmoil. There were more takeovers and breweries were run by the slide rule and balance sheet. Keg beer was thrust upon the public, who were told that this is what they wanted. CAMRA was formed to fight what must have seemed a losing battle. The Coventry and Mid-Warwickshire branch produced the *Warwickshire Real Beer Guide*. It was a slim work of barely nineteen pages and it told a sorry story. Ansell's and M&B dominated throughout the county, with glimmers of hope from such breweries as Hook Norton and Ruddles, who supplied obscure pubs that the big boys had been unable to find and take over. Stifle your tears, put away your hankies – help was at hand. The 1980s saw the unstoppable rise of the micro-brewery. There were hiccups and splutters and some fell by the wayside, but by the 1990s the micro-brewery was firmly established. *What's Brewing* announced their arrivals, a dozen or more each year. Their beers had daft names, which sometimes left you embarrassed when you ordered one, but what great joy there was at this choice and variety. It was a choice that our grandfathers would have known before the mergers and takeovers. As a beer drinker, it is a wonderful time to be alive and no more so than in Warwickshire.

Joseph McKenna
September 2005

ONE

EARLY AND DOMESTIC BREWING

Concerning its early brewing history, Warwickshire is fortunate in having detailed records for both Coventry and Stratford-upon-Avon. These records, to a greater or lesser extent, reflect the early history of brewing throughout the county. In 1493 the Coventry Leet Book, the official administrative record of the city, named six of its common brewers. As they drew their water for brewing from the common supply, they were obliged to pay an additional water rate. Their names and rates were accordingly listed. These early brewers included:

Thos. Bredon be yere	*Xiijs iiiid*
Ric. Jackson be yere	*Xijs iiijd*
Nic. Burwey be yere	*Xs*
Ric. Drake	*Vs viijd*
Rob. Mason	*Viijs iiijd*
Heddes wyfe	*Vjs viijd*

In addition, Roger Wade, a dyer, is also listed. There is a suggestion that there were other brewers not included. The Leet Book records: 'Also hit was ordeyned … that all ye persons whos names [appear] and all other that can be founde within this citie that brue to sale … and they that theire names be not here they to be rated be ye Maire and his Counceill'. Certainly by 1508 there were a sufficient number of brewers in the city to form a Brewers' Guild. By 1520 the Leet Book records that there were sixty-eight common brewers, each using on average 146 quarters and 1 bushel of malt a week to brew their ale. In 1537, when Christopher Waid was mayor, the council made strenuous efforts to regulate the brewing and selling of ale. The Leet Book for 7 July 1537 ordained:

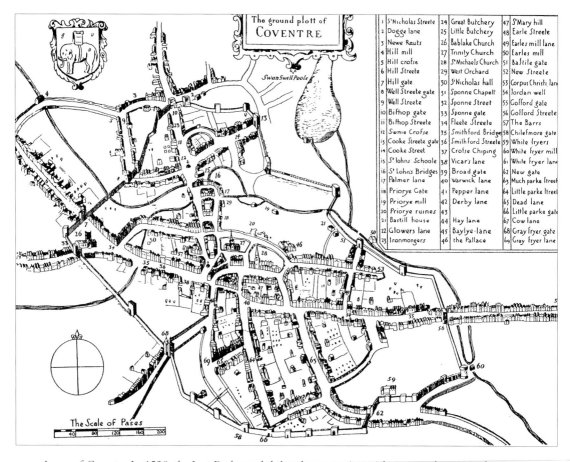

The ground plott of **COVENTRE**

1	St Nicholas Streete	24	Great Butchery	47	St Mary hill
2	Dogge lane	25	Little Butchery	48	Earle Streete
3	Newe Reuts	26	Bablake Church	49	Earles mill lane
4	Hill mill	27	Trinity Church	50	Earles mill
5	Hill crofse	28	St Michaels Church	51	Baftile gate
6	Hill Streete	29	West Orchard	52	New Streete
7	Hill gate	30	St Nicholas hall	53	Corpus Christi lane
8	Well Streete gate	31	Sponne Chapell	54	Jordan well
9	Well Streete	32	Sponne Street	55	Gofford gate
10	Bifhop gate	33	Sponne gate	56	Golford Streete
11	Bifhop Streete	34	Fleete Streete	57	The Barrs
12	Swnie Crofse	35	Smithford Bridge	58	Chilefmore gate
13	Cooke Streete gate	36	Smithford Streete	59	White fryers
14	Cooke Street	37	Crofse Chiping	60	White fryer mill
15	St Johns Schoole	38	Vicar's lane	61	White fryer lane
16	St Johns Bridges	39	Broad gate	62	New gate
17	Palmer lane	40	Warwick lane	63	Much parke ftreet
18	Priorye Gate	41	Pepper lane	64	Little parke ftreet
19	Priorye mill	42	Derby lane	65	Dead lane
20	Priorye ruines	43		66	Little parke gate
21	Bastill house	44	Hay lane	67	Cow lane
22	Glowers lane	45	Baylye-lane	68	Gray fryer gate
23	Ironmongers	46	the Pallace	69	Gray fryer lane

The Scale of Pases

A map of Coventry. In 1520, the Leet Book recorded that there were sixty-eight common brewers in the city.

That all the Brewers of this Citie, which brewe to sell, shall sell ther newe ale after the rait of xviijd the Cester [there being 14 gallons to the cester], upon peyn to forfeit for every defau[l]t to the Shireffes of the Citie vjs viijd.

Item, that all reteyllers & tipplers of ale of this Citie shall sell there ale by reteyll after the rait ensuing, That is to say, the best stale ale dronke owt of the house for ijd the galon, and within the house for iijd the galon: And that the said Tiplers shall ordeyn & make ther pottes & measures after the raites abovesaid within x dayes next ensuying this presente lete, upone peyn to forfeit for every defaute vjs viijd to the use aforseid.

It was decided that every Alderman in his ward should elect two Ale Tasters to enforce this order.

Over the following years, brewing became highly lucrative and many left their old trades to become brewers and ale-house owners, much to the disservice of the city, which lost skilled artisans. In 1544 the mayor and council called in all licences and ordained that, from Easter Sunday, no inhabitant of the city:

shall frome & after the Feast of Penticost … brewe or tipple eny ale within this Citie to sell but onlie suche person & persones as shal-be appointed, named & licenced by Maister Meyre & the Justices of the peace of this Citie … upon peyne to forfeit xls [£10].

At Stratford-upon-Avon, in 1557, the council decided upon the price that beer and ale should be sold. New beer was to be sold at inns throughout the town, in a registered size of pot, at 2d a gallon; 2d a gallon was the price for stale, or old, ale and 1d for 2 gallons of small or weak beer. This type of beer would have been drunk by everyone, children included, in place of water, it being pure and free from disease. All ale had to be tested by the Ale Tasters before sale, under pain of a fine of 20s per brew. Even as late as 1558, the council still forbade the use of hops in beer within the borough, though they had become acceptable in London-brewed beer by 1534. That same year, 1558, the council forbade people from becoming common brewers without the consent of the said council. Those discovered doing so were liable to a £10 fine. A clear division between common brewers and victuallers, or inn holders, was legally established in 1564, the year of Shakespeare's birth. Incidentally, Shakespeare's father at one time acted as an Ale Taster. Brewers were not permitted to sell their beer direct to the public. This was the preserve of the retail trade or 'common tipplers'. By 1598, however, the 'tipplers' were abusing their position by brewing their own 'unreasonable stronge drincke', which led 'to the encrease of quarrelinge and other misdemeaneres'. Beer and ale, it was ordered, would henceforward have to be bought from the common brewers, thus redressing the balance and better enabling the authorities to regulate the strength of beer sold. To increase commerce, the common brewers were forbidden to grind their own malt, but were ordered to take it to the common mills of the town. Thus the production and distribution of beer and ale was better regulated to the overall advantage of the town and its tradesmen.

Stratford-upon-Avon. In 1557, the town council regulated the brewing of ale.

Some years later, in 1667, the probate inventory of James Russhen, innkeeper of Solihull, was drawn up following his death. He was landlord of the Bell, now renamed the George Hotel, overlooking the parish church of St Alphege. As well as an innkeeper, he was also a brewer and maltster. The main room of his house, the hall, was used as a dining room, while his parlour had a more relaxed ambience, with half a dozen chairs and cushions, and a coal fire burning in the hearth. Russhen ground his malt in his own mill-house, and in his buttery there were twelve hogsheads and barrels 'with beer in the same'. A hogshead held 52½ gallons, or 630 pints. In seventeenth-century Warwickshire the brew house was also known as a yeeling house – the house where brewing took place. It was a vat house or place where wort was put to ferment during the brewing process.

In 1670 Thomas King was appointed lord mayor of the city of Coventry. He was re-appointed in 1691. Surviving records show that he bought the Rose & Crown in High Street in 1692, and in 1699 he bought the Turk's Head in Little Park Street, from William Gilbert. King died in 1702. Other municipally minded brewers include Edward Rawson, whom Benjamin Poole in his *History of Coventry,* published in 1870, describes as 'an eminent brewer'. In 1704 he caused a new waterworks to be constructed from a spring outside Bishop Gate, and its water conducted by pipes to his brew house in Cow Lane. This water supply, which cost him £370 to provide, he shared with his neighbours. In 1724 Joseph Ash, who had fallen foul of the authorities in 1684 for brewing without permission, was elected to the office of Chamberlain. Brewing in Coventry had become respectable.

In 1756 there were 127 public houses in Coventry, according to Alderman Hewitt's journal. By this time, there were no known common brewers in the city, so it would appear that these, in the main, were home-brew houses. Accounts for this period at Coventry Record Office refer to brew houses, but these appear to be public houses or domestic brewers. It was not until 1801 that Coventry gained what we would look upon today as a common brewer. The firm, designating itself the Coventry Brewery, was established in Leicester Row, by the partnership of William Summerfield and David Lloyd, of the well-known Birmingham banking family. By 1808 the enterprise was known as the Coventry Porter Brewery, Joseph Owen being added to the partnership of Summerfield, Lloyd & Owen. Apparently struggling, it was taken over by Joseph Phillips & Son, and somehow, despite hiccups and amalgamations, survived until 1912.

James Russhen's 1667 Bell Inn (now the George Hotel), Solihull.

TWO

RETAIL BREWERS AND HOME-BREW HOUSES

With a few exceptions – Coventry most notably – the Warwickshire inn dates from the post-Reformation period. Previously, the needs of the traveller and pilgrim were met by the religious houses. With their destruction from 1534 onwards, domestic houses were converted into public houses, to cater for the needs of the traveller. In many cases, beer would have been brewed on the premises. Brewing was originally the province of the woman of the house, so with the rise of the inn we find that brewing by them is carried over into the public sector. At Stratford we find such women as Agnes Samwell (1554) and Alice Nevell (1560). At the Bowling Green, in Leamington, Margaret Walsgave was listed as a brewer in 1625. Brewing was also carried on by the old. The Coventry Leet Book of 1622 complained that:

> the Trades of Maulting, brewing and victualing by manie Straungers, fforreyners in this Citie and Suburbs thereof (not being ffreemen) hath beene a great hindrance and damage to many of the poore Citizens, ffreemen of this Citie, using the same Trades in tyme of theire older age and decay of theire Trades.

In Warwickshire the home-brew house survived well into the twentieth century. The Blue Bell at Waring's Green, in the old parish of Tanworth-in-Arden, just south-west of Solihull, was brewing up to 1968 and has the distinction of being not only the county's last home-brew pub but also, following its takeover by Bulmer's, the county's only cider house.

The Duke of Wellington's Beerhouse Act of 1830, introduced in an effort to wean people away from the evils of drinking Holland gin, abolished the duty on beer and made it possible for anyone with two guineas to spare to obtain a licence from the Commissioners of Excise to brew and sell good English beer. In the industrial areas of the West Midlands many eagerly seized the chance. In Birmingham in the first two years of the Act's existence, 116 retail breweries were established. In the Black Country this figure rose to 146. In Warwickshire, however, very few people seem to have taken the advantage of establishing new businesses. In Leamington, comparable in size with Wolverhampton, only four people are listed as retail brewers by 1832; this in comparison with Wolverhampton's seventy-five brewers. In Coventry, Warwick and Stratford the figures are negligible. The local village pub seems to have served the needs of the people, and by and large the county does not have the reputation, as with the Black Country, of being a harsh place with hard drinkers. In addition, even as late as 1841, communal brew houses were still being built. A brew house was built by Squire Gumley Wilson to serve a row of seven terraced cottages in Wilson's Row, Knowle. It still exists, situated between the right-hand end of the row and Milverton Crescent. There is a plaque on the wall bearing his initials and the date, 1841. In 1984 a planning application was put in to Solihull Council to demolish the brew house and replace it with a modern house. Strong pressure against such a move saw the application turned down.

The Beerhouse Act was modified in 1840 and repealed in 1869, following protest from common brewers and publicans. Beerhouses continued to exist until the 1950s, though to all intents and purposes they had become public houses. The following list is a compilation of retail and home-brew houses, compiled from a variety of sources.

ALCESTER

Angel Inn, 4-5 Church Street. A home-brew house during the tenancy of the Overbury family in the early nineteenth century. They also produced ginger beer.

Bell Inn Brewery, George Henry Woodfield, 1923-26. Home-brew house, but Woodfield may have supplied the free trade.

Bull's Head Brewery, Three Tuns, 34 High Street. Founded originally at Inkberrow in December 1994 but moved to the rear of the Three Tuns in 1995. It supplied the pub with a limited number of beers, including Light (ABV 4.5%). Closed down in 1996.

Dog & Partridge, Bleachfield Street. Formerly the King's Head under Samuel Townsend, it had become the Dog & Partridge by 1811. The local newspaper, the *Alcester Chronicle*, advertised the sale of the inn's brewing plant in April 1898, indicating that brewing on the premises had ceased by that date.

Golden Lion, 57 Priory Road. Established as a beerhouse by 1851 under Joseph Tarkle, who was also a brewer. A sales catalogue for 1894 indicates that brewing had by then ceased, as it refers to the 'former brewing buildings'. The house was later acquired by Flowers.

Oak Inn, Radford Road. John Staite was licensee and brewer in 1872.

The Roebuck, Birmingham Road. Built around 1827. A sales notice of 1892 advertised that it included a brewing plant. The pub was later taken over by Flowers.

Rose & Crown, 15 Evesham Street. Originating in 1792 under licensee and victualler William Garfield. A sales catalogue of 1909 refers to it as an 'old established, fully licensed inn' with a 'smoke room, bar, front tap room, private sitting room, 4 large bedrooms, kitchen, brew house, cellar'. The Rose & Crown closed in the late 1960s.

The Swan, Swan Street. A sixteenth-century house rebuilt in the eighteenth century, its earliest known licensee was Thomas Harryngton, in 1598. The probate inventory of John Bovey for 1730 lists a brew house.

Turk's Head, High Street. William Russen is listed as licensee and brewer from 1868 until 1878. Though essentially a home-brew pub, it did also supply the free trade.

White Lion, Evesham Street. A home-brew house dating back to 1715, when Edward Crow was licensee. The records of the petty sessions for 1872 reveal that the house included a parlour, kitchen, bar, smoke room, brew house, cellar and six bedrooms. The White Lion was rebuilt in 1932, when brewing apparently ceased.

Henry George Woodfield, 1914–21.

ASHOW

Richard Winsmore, Brewer & Baker, 1595-1620.

ASTLEY

Edwin Allen, 1923.

ATHERSTONE

Augustine J. Trivett, 1914-23.

BEDWORTH

British Queen, Bulkington Lane. A home-brew house bought up by the Leamington Brewery.

White Horse, Bedworth Road. A home-brew house later acquired by the Leamington Brewery.

BRAILES

P. & F. Taylor Brothers. Originated in 1899 and situated next door to its brewery tap, the Gate Inn. Though now closed, and the building converted to other uses, it is just possible to make out the faded painted sign, 'Brailes Brewery'. It closed in 1906.

BUBBENHALL

The Horseshoes. Thomas Walton, 1845. Brewer and licensee.

BULKINGTON

White Lion. A former home-brew house. Charles Dalton was landlord and brewer, 1864-68.

CLAVERDON

Red Lion. A home-brew house. James Aston, a farmer, was landlord here from 1884-92.

COLESHILL

Coach & Horses, High Street. William H. Farrin is listed as licensee and brewer in 1845.

John Hextall, Park Road, 1914-33.

Robert Hextall, Park Road, 1934-40.

John James Simms, High Street, 1914-23.

Three Horse Shoes, Lower High Street, late nineteenth century and early twentieth century. Brewers of 'Pure Home Brewed Ales'.

COUGHTON

Thomas Whitcher, 1864.

COVENTRY

Mr Arsle, brewer, was fined for leaving rubbish in front of his house in 1719.

Alice and Joseph Ash. Mother and son were indicted for brewing beer without a licence in January and October 1684. In 1720 Ash, then a respectable brewer and landowner, gave to his son, Joseph Jr, the present of two public houses and a malthouse, upon his marriage to Bridget Sterges. Joseph Jr brewed until around 1785; he is not listed in Bailey's Western Directory of that year.

Sidney Athersuch, The Recruiting Sergeant, 14 Spon Street, 1914. John Athersuch, 1923. Mrs Sarah Athersuch, 1926.

Thomas Bailey, Samson & Lion, 34 Swanswell Terrace, 1914.

William Henry Batchelor, Hop Pole Brewery, Hop Pole Inn, 16 Leicester Row, 1903-14.

Joseph Bickley, O Rare Ben Johnson, 18 New Street, 1914.

Henry Brown, Spon Street Brewery, 1864-67. Also a wine and spirit merchant.

Mrs Mary Clara Brown, Blue Bell, Greyfriars Lane, 1914-20.

Buck & Crown, Bond Street. A noted home-brew house in the late nineteenth century.

Bull's Head, Bishop Street. A home-brew pub later taken over by the Leamington Brewery.

Thomas Burns, Old Bull & Anchor Yard, Bishop Street, 1896.

Frederick William Burr, Five Ways Tavern, 61 Harnall Lane, 1914-20.

Henry Causer, Malt Shovel, 93 Spon End, 1914.

Thomas Claridge, Lamp Tavern, 13 Cook Street, 1921-30.

Joseph Cross, 10 Cross Cheaping, 1914.

Crow in the Oak, Lockhurst Lane. A home-brew house, late nineteenth and early twentieth centuries.

Hubert Duggins, 51 Yardley Street, 1914. Mrs Florence Duggins, 1921.

Mrs Emma Ellen Faulconbridge, 19 Tower Street, 1914-20.

Fox Inn, College Square. A home-brew house.

Mrs Lizzie Garbutt, 23 Albion Street, 1914.

Elizabeth Gray, Cross Keys, Earl Street, 1850.

SPON STREET BREWERY & LIQUOR VAULTS, COVENTRY.

JOHN SODEN,

ALE AND PORTER BREWER,

DEALER IN WINES AND SPIRITS,

Auctioneer, Appraiser, & House Agent.

APPOINTED AGENT FOR MESSRS. WOOD AND CO.'S

CELEBRATED LONDON PORTER AND STOUT.

SUPERIOR HOME BREWED ALES & BEER,

In Casks from $4\frac{1}{2}$ Gallons to 36 Gallons each, at prices from 6d. per Gallon to 1s. 6d.

ORDERS ADDRESSED TO

SPON STREET BREWERY

WILL HAVE IMMEDIATE ATTENTION.

An advertisement for John Soden's Spon Street Brewery, later taken over by Henry Brown.

The Malt Shovel, Spon End, Coventry.

> JAMES THOMPSON,
> NAG'S HEAD INN,
> SPON END,
> COVENTRY.
>
> Home Brewed Ales and Wines and Spirits of the best qualities; Large Yard, Good Stabling, Lock-up Coach House, &c.
>
> THOMAS NORTH,
> MALT SHOVEL,
> SPON END.
>
> HOME BREWED ALES & WINES & SPIRITS OF THE BEST QUALITY.

Advertisements for nineteenth-century Coventry home-brew houses.

John Hall, 37 George Street, 1866.

James Heale, Spon Street, 1839.

Mrs Annie Hewitt, 35 Smithford Street, 1914-20.

Frank Hewitt, 60 Castle Street, 1914-21. Alfred Hewitt, 1923.

Frederick Hewitt, Leopard, 38 Primrose Hill Street, 1914.

R. Higgitt, Brewer & Baker, 89 East Street, 1860.

Edward John Hollins, 48 Spon Street, 1866.

John Jordan, Bishop Street, 1835. Retail brewer. Later moved into the trade of maltster, wine and spirit merchant, corn and coal merchant, by 1845.

Mr King, brewer, left rubbish in the street near his home in 1719. He was fined accordingly. This may well be the son of Thomas King, below.

Thomas King, brewer, was appointed mayor of Coventry in 1670 and 1691. In 1692 he purchased the Rose & Crown in High Street. He bought the Turk's Head in 1699. King was dead by 1703, when his wife acted on his behalf.

Thomas Kirby, 45 Cox Street, and stores at 39 New Street, 1914-20.

Thomas Love, Smithford Street, 1679-99.

Joseph Manton, brewer, 1788.

W. Martin, Butchers Arms. A home-brew house.

John J. Mattocks, Golden Cup, 35 Far Gosford Street, 1914.

Charles Mitchener, 17 Whitefriars Lane, 1914-21.

Thomas North, Malt Shovel, Spon End, 1890.

Old Windmill Inn, Spon Street. Popularly known as 'Ma' Brown's in tribute to its long-serving landlady. This is a seventeenth-century home-brew house, with brewing continuing here up to the beginning of the twentieth century. The brew house at the rear has survived, though seating has extended into it.

Mrs Lucy Overton, 49 East Street, 1914-23.

Thomas Owen, brewer, 1792.

Thomas Paybody, 17 Radford Road, 1914-20.

William Perkins, Stoke Green, Stoke, 1872.

Priory Tavern, New Building. A home-brew house.

Rainbow Inn and Brewery, 73 Birmingham Road, Allesley. A home-brew pub that began brewing in 1994 with a 2-barrel plant. In 1996 this was upgraded to a 4-barrel plant.

Edward Rawson, Cow Lane. Described as 'an eminent brewer' in Poole's *History of Coventry*, 1870. He erected at his own expense a new work at a spring outside Bishop Gate, which conducted its water by pipes to his brew house. The project cost £370.

Red House Inn, Stoney Stanton Road. Thomas Venn was licensee and brewer in 1878. The pub also had pleasure gardens attached.

William Sagar, Meriden Tavern, 64 New Buildings, 1914.

Mrs Mary Ann Sidwell, 26 Cromwell Street, Red Lane, 1914-20.

George Taylor, Townwall Tavern, Bond Street, 1914.

James Thompson, Nag's Head Inn, Spon End, 1890. Hope & Anchor, 38 Sherbourne Street, 1914. Both were home-brew houses.

John Thomas Thorpe, 42 New Street, 1914-20.

J.E. Thursby, British Queen Inn, St John's Street.

Above: *One of the ales produced by the Butchers Arms in Coventry, a home-brew house.*

Right: *The remains of the Victorian brewery at the Old Windmill, Coventry.*

Below: *The Old Windmill, Spon Street, Coventry, a home-brew house.*

The Town Wall Tavern in Coventry, a home-brew house.

The Mother Huff Cap, Great Alne.

Mrs Catherine Edith Twyneham, 23 Spon Street, 1914–30.

Thomas Venn, Stoney Stanton Road, 1876–78.

Arthur Wareham, Hope & Anchor, 17 Whitefriars Lane, 1923.

William Waters, brewer, 1851.

Fred Watson, Old Chase, 42 Gosford Street, 1914.

Thomas Webbe, brewer of Bishop Street, 1522. He appears in the muster roll of that year.

R. Willoughby, Star Brewery, 21 West Orchard, 1894–96. Cooper and brewer.

James Wormwood, St Nicholas Place, 1839.

FENNY COMPTON

George & Dragon, Fenny Compton Wharf. Also at Byfield. Richard Guest Brown was landlord in 1878. Robert Brown was landlord from 1880–84, and Richard Brown from 1888–90.

FOLESHILL

J. Jones, Little Heath, 1850. This may be the origin of Michael Spencer's Rock Brewery. (*see* Home-brewed (Coventry) Ltd)

GREAT ALNE

Mother Huff Cap Inn. A seventeenth-century home-brew house. During the late nineteenth and early twentieth centuries they brewed a very strong Huff Cap Ale here.

HARBOROUGH MAGNA

Golden Lion. A home-brew house, run by Thomas Bird in 1880.

HUNNINGHAM

Red Lion. Barnacle's Brewery. A home-brew house originating in 1845, under brewer John Barnacle. It closed in 1876.

KENILWORTH

Bowling Green Inn, Abbey Hill. A home-brew house under John Phillips in 1866. Phillips also sold Burton Ales, beer from Joule's of Stone, and Guinness.

The Wyandotte. A home-brew house under the Wilkinson family until 1946. Now a Marston's house.

LAPWORTH

The Boot. A home-brew house dating back to the early eighteenth century. The probate inventory of licensee Thomas Sly, who died in 1722, lists a brew house attached to his premises.

An advertisement for the Bowling Green Inn in Kenilworth, a home-brew house.

LEAMINGTON SPA

J. Barnacle, Hunningham, 1872.

R. Bartlam, Kenilworth Street, 1830. Retail brewer.

Bowling Green, High Street. A home-brew house dating back to 1625. Margaret Walsgrave was licensee.

Castle Hotel, Brunswick Street. A home-brew house in operation by 1825. The hotel and its brewery had closed by 1850.

The Dog, High Street. A home-brew house dating back to 1625, when William Mills was licensee.

William Dutton, Kenilworth Street, 1830. Retail brewer.

John Edgerton, 29 Chandos Street, 1914.

Golden Lion, Regent Street. James Miles was licensee in 1812, when the house was put up for sale. The sale details reveal that the pub had a 'large brew house and excellent cellarage'.

John Hanson, Binswood Street, 1830. Retail brewer.

King's Arms, Warwick Street. A home-brew house. R. Dee was brewer and licensee in 1835.

Newmarket Inn, Tavistock Street. J. Coult is listed as licensee and brewer in 1835.

Oak Inn, Radford Road. John Staite was listed as a brewer here from 1868 to 1884. He is also listed as an auctioneer, maltster, hop merchant, brewer and corn factor. The brewery closed around 1888, when Staite became a full-time auctioneer. The pub still survives as an Ansell's house.

Henry Parsonage, 2 Tavistock Street. 1868.

A.W. Philpotts, 29 Chandos Street, 1921.

John Sewell, 7 Vincent Street, 1866.

John Staite, Radford Road, 1868-88.

William Stuchfield, Tavistock Street, 1830. Retail brewer.

J. Young, 45 King Street, 1864.

Williams's Directory Advertiser.

J. W. BAKER,

ALE & PORTER BREWER,

Castle Brewery, Leamington,

Continues to supply his much esteemed ALES and PORTER,
at the undermentioned prices:—viz.

	ALE				*PORTER*		
X.	1	0 per Gallon.		XP.	1	0 per Gallon.
XX.	1	4 ,,	,,	XXP.	1	4 ,,	,,
XXX.	1	8 ,,	,,	XXXP.	1	8 ,,	,,

FINE OLD ALE

1s. 5d. and 1s. 9d. per Gallon.

EAST INDIA PALE ALE

One and Fourpence per Gallon.

In Casks, containing $4\frac{1}{2}$, 9, 18, or 36 Gallons each.

*Parties requiring TABLE BEER, are requested to order it
at least, ten days before required for use, as no Beer is kept in
store at a lower price than One Shilling per Gallon.*

BOTTLED ALE OR PORTER,

IN QUART BOTTLES.				IN PINT BOTTLES.		
	s.	d.			s.	d.
XX.	5	0 per dozen		XX.	3	9 per dozen.
XXX.	6	0 ,, ,,		XXX.	4	6 ,, ,,

In quantities not less than two dozen Quarts or four
dozen Pints.

The usual discount allowed to Hotel and Innkeepers.

Above: *An 1846 price list for the Castle Brewery in Leamington.*

Opposite: *An advertisement for the Bull's Head in Meriden, 1866.*

MERIDEN

William Boden, Bull's Head, 'Fine Home-brewed Ales', 1866.

MIDDLE TYSOE

John Henry Middleton, brewer at Church Farm, 1876-1892.

MONKS KIRBY

The Bell. Home-brew house, 1896-98, under C. Pelton Sanson. Arthur Rhead became licensee and brewer in 1899. Ceased brewing in 1912.

Denbigh Arms. Home-brew house, listed as such from 1880. John T. Bird, a farmer, was its long-term brewer. Basil Hewitt took over the premises in 1887. James Edward Lea was its last brewer, taking over the licence in 1889. Brewing ceased in 1921.

NEWBOLD-ON-AVON

Marcus Lowe, 1880-1900.

NEWTON REGIS

Thomas Bail, aged twenty-six, listed as a brewer in the 1851 census.

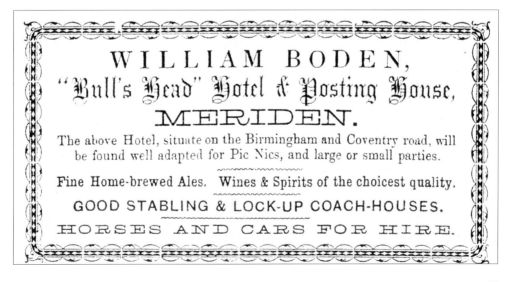

WILLIAM BODEN,
"Bull's Head" Hotel & Posting House,
MERIDEN.

The above Hotel, situate on the Birmingham and Coventry road, will be found well adapted for Pic Nics, and large or small parties.

Fine Home-brewed Ales. Wines & Spirits of the choicest quality.

GOOD STABLING & LOCK-UP COACH-HOUSES.

HORSES AND CARS FOR HIRE.

NUNEATON

Castle Inn, Market Place. Thomas Benfield, licensee and brewer, 1854-64.

Thomas Cooper & Co., 8 Abbey Street, 1900-14.

Crystal Palace (formerly the Hare & Squirrel), Market Place. A home-brew house later taken over by the Leamington Brewery.

Thomas Salt & Co., 8 Abbey Street, 1923-26.

PAILTON

The Fox. Home-brew house. Josiah Cox was listed as brewer here in 1896.

QUINTON

Thomas Green, Moor Street, 1923.

RUGBY

Eyre & Co., 16 St James Street. David Lilley was the company agent in 1874.

Victoria Inn, Victoria Brewery, North Street. Marcus Lowe, brewer, 1874-1892. Address alternatively given as Lower Hillmorton Road.

SALTER STREET

Bull's Head, on the corner of Limekiln Lane. A former home-brew house, allegedly dating from 1740. Architecturally the pub and brewery are Victorian, dating from around 1854. They were built by farmer John Smith, who is listed as a 'farmer and beer retailer of Salter Street'. In 1878 Richard Busby bought the house and brewery. He was succeeded by Edward Paddy in 1885. Thomas Hill, who was also a farmer, took over the beerhouse in 1892 and ran it in conjunction with his farm until 1918. William Walters then took it over and during his tenancy, in 1935, it became the Bull's Head. The house and brewery were taken over by Ansell's and brewing ceased. The brewery, a small two-and-a-half-storey tower brewery attached to the pub, still survives. The ground floor has been converted into pub use. The Bull's Head is now a Thwaites house.

SHIPSTON-ON-STOUR

Robert Berry, maltster and brewer, Husbandman's End, 1854.

The Bull's Head in Salter Street, a mid-nineteenth-century home-brew house. The brewery is centre left in the photograph.

Black Horse Inn. Home-brew house, first licensed to brew ale in 1540. Also known in the early twentieth century for its home-made parsnip, rhubarb and cowslip wines. Brewing ceased around 1940.

Feldon Brewery, Coach & Horses, 16 New Street. Brewing commenced at the pub in 1996 but was suspended following renovations in 1997. Subsequently, brewer Bob Payne died and the Coach & Horses is now a Hook Norton house. The Feldon Brewery produced two beers, FB1 (Feldon Brewery First Brew) and At Last.

SNITTERFIELD

Bell Inn. Thomas Grant was licensee in 1896.

Snitterfield Brewery. Thomas Grant's Bell Inn brewery. Kelly's Directory of Warwickshire in 1896 listed 'Thomas Grant, Bell Inn, brewer & maltster; accommodation for parties & picnics &c., stabling & posting'.

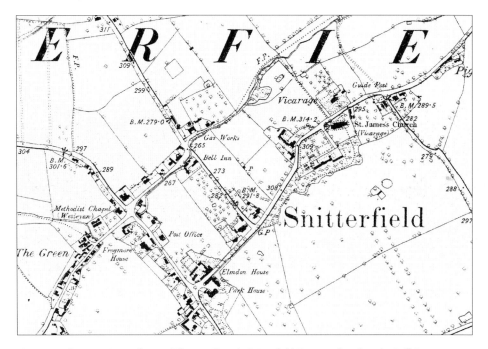

A nineteenth-century map showing Thomas Grant's Snitterfield Brewery, based at the Bell Inn.

SOLIHULL

Barley Mow, at the junction of Poplar Road and Warwick Road. Sarah Penny was the licensee in 1851. Her son William was brewer. John Chinn was publican and brewer from 1870 to 1872.

Dutton & Hudson, High Street, 1900.

Gardeners' Arms, High Street. A home-brew house opened in the early 1860s. It took its name from its first licensee, James Bridge, who was a keen gardener. William Lines brewed here from 1892 to 1935. By 1914 he was the sole brewer in Solihull. The old house was demolished in 1971.

Thomas Hood, 23 High Street. Brewer and maltster, 1851-68.

James Russhen, brewer and landlord of the Bell (now the George Hotel). According to his probate inventory of 1667, in the buttery were twelve hogsheads and barrels with 'beer in the same'. This would be the equivalent of 630 gallons.

Henry Lee, High Street, 1845. Maltster and brewer.

George Wall, High Street, 1868.

J. Whitehouse, 1864.

The Barley Mow in Solihull was built on the site of the earlier house of the same name. William Penney was brewer here in 1851.

The Gardeners Arms, Solihull, a home-brew pub.

Henry Lee's Mason's Arms, Solihull. It was a home-brew house.

STONELEIGH

Sarah Hale, aged seventy-two, listed as a brewer in the 1851 census.

Thomas Hall, brewer at 'the inn' in Stoneleigh, 1605. He was succeeded by his son, Thomas Jr, in 1620.

Robert Heartland, grocer, provision dealer, brewer and beer retailer, 1872.

STRATFORD-UPON-AVON

Robert Ballamy, brewer, 1560.

George and Richard Banester, common brewers, 1558.

John Beesley, Rother Market, 1830. Brewer and cordwainer (shoemaker).

William Brace, brewer, 1560.

Henry Clifford, 36 Wood Street, 1866. Brewer and greengrocer.

George E. Court, 21 Church Street, 1914-20.

The old brewery at the rear of the Lamp Lighter (formerly the Seven Stars), Stratford-upon-Avon. John Beesley brewed here in 1830.

George Court's Windmill Brewery, Church Street, Stratford-upon-Avon. The house was later taken over by Flowers.

Cross Keys. J. Austin, wholesale and retail brewer, 1866.

William Eborall, 1 Mansell Street, 1914-26.

William Gibbs, 1 Warwick Road, 1914-21.

William Guy, 49 Russell Street. Innkeeper and brewer, 1851.

Hitchman & Co., 17 Church Street, 1900-08.

Thomas Holtom. Accused in 1556 of selling his beer before it had been tested by the Ale Tasters.

Thomas Hunt, brewer, 1560.

John Ichiver, Henley Street, 1561. Brewer and town Ale Taster.

Roger London, brewer, 1560.

Robert Mylles, brewer, 1560.

John Nevell, brewer, 1554. Alice Nevell, 1560.

Plymouth Arms, Wood Street. A home-brew house. Moses Hands was licensee and brewer in 1866.

Rose Inn, 14 Ely Street. A home-brew house under John Alcock in 1866.

Thomas Rychardson, brewer, 1560.

Robert Salesbury. He was taken to court in 1556 for producing and selling unwholesome ale.

An advertisement for Austin's Cross Keys, Stratford-upon-Avon.

The Cross Keys, Stratford-upon-Avon, a home-brew house under J. Austin.

The Odd Fellows Arms, Mansell Street, Stratford-upon-Avon. William Eborall's 1920s brewery is to the right.

"ROSE" INN,

ELY STREET,

STRATFORD-ON-AVON.

JOHN ALCOCK,

PROPRIETOR.

Families supplied with Home-Brewed Ales on the most reasonable terms.

MOSES HANDS,

Brewer, Corn Merchant, &c.,

"PLYMOUTH ARMS,"

WOOD STREET, STRATFORD-ON-AVON.

POST HORSES ON THE SHORTEST NOTICE.

Good Stabling and Lock-up Coach Houses.

Commercial Travellers, Excursionists, and others visiting Stratford, will find excellent accommodation at the above House, at moderate charges.

CHOICE WINES AND SPIRITS.

Families supplied with Home Brewed Ales and Banbury Porter, in Casks, from 9 gallons upwards.

An 1866 advertisement for the Rose Inn, Stratford-upon-Avon.

Agnes Samwell, brewster, 1554.

Peter Smart, brewer, 1560.

Stratford Arms, 39 Henley Street. Charles Daniel, 'Fine Home-Brewed Ales', 1866.

Henry Sydnall, brewer, 1560.

Alfred Wall, Falstaff Brewery, Henley Street, 1880.

STUDLEY

Barley Mow, Studley Brewery. A home-brew house with brewery to the rear. It ceased brewing around 1875.

WARINGS GREEN

John Lucas, Blue Bell Brewery. A Georgian public house, situated alongside the Stratford-upon-Avon Canal. The two-storey Victorian brewery behind was built by John Bladen around 1854. Bladen was succeeded as publican by Thomas Powell (1864-66); William Fardon, a former beer retailer from Hockley Heath (1867-73); John Hobeche (1878); Joseph Green (1880-92); and Joseph Stephenson, who was also a farmer (1896-1901). In 1901 John W. Lucas bought the pub and brewery. Upon his death, his widow Laura ran the business until her death in 1966, at the age of ninety-four. She was succeeded by her son Laurence, who died two years later in 1968. The house was then sold to cider makers Bulmer's of Hereford, and the brewing of beer ceased. The brewery building still survives but its ground floor has been converted to other uses. Although it is primarily a cider house, the Blue Bell also sells beer, much of which comes from the smaller breweries.

The Stratford Arms in Henley Street was a home-brew house in nineteenth-century Stratford-upon-Avon.

WARWICK

Dennis Aucott, 40 Brook Street, 1920.

Ernest John Barratt, 50 Friars Street, 1914-20.

Walter W. Clarke, The Brewery, Coventry Road, 1904-06.

Emscote Tavern, 102 Emscote Road. Listed in the directories as a home-brew house under W.J. Marshall in 1896. In 1902 John Upton took over the pub and brewery and ran it up to 1928. Brewing appears to have ended in 1904, when Upton went to work as a representative for Birmingham brewers Davenport's. The Emscote Tavern later became an Ansell's tied house.

Gold Cup, Castle Street. A home-brew house under John Teague in 1866. The pub, a regular rendezvous of 'old gaffers' who drank mild and smoked their pipes, has now become a trendy wine bar.

Thomas Enoch Illiffe, 1 Birmingham Road, 1914-20.

James B. McCartney, Priory Road, 1914.

The Blue Bell, Waring's Green.

Lucas' Brewery at the rear of the Blue Bell.

Millwright Arms, 67 Coten End. A micro-brewery at the rear of the pub was established in December 1997. In the summer of 1998 brewing ceased upon the instructions of Punch Taverns, owner of the Millwright Arms. The brewing plant was subsequently removed.

William Job Power, Saltisford, 1914-21.

Thomas Smith, 1 High Street. Listed in the 1851 census as a brewer from Tachbrook.

William Whyte, Woolpack Hotel, Market Place, 1873. A home-brew house.

Woodman Brewery, Priory Road. James B. MacCartney brewed his MacCartney Ales here from 1896 until his death in 1920.

WOLFHAMCOTE

Joseph Gibbs, aged forty-one, appears in the 1851 census as a brewer.

WOLVEY

William Bates, brewer and maltster, 1874-92.

WOOTTON WAWEN

John Hoitt, brewer and victualler, 1830.

SPENNELL'S WARWICK ENTERPRISE ALMANACK AND DIRECTORY.   273

WOOLPACK HOTEL,

First-Class Family & Commercial,

(Newly Furnished and under New Management,)

MARKET PLACE, WARWICK.
WM. WHYTE.

Marriage Breakfasts, Dinners, Ball Suppers, &c.,
PURVEYED FOR.

BILLIARDS.   LOOSE BOXES.

WOOLPACK HOTEL

Wine and Spirit Stores,

MARKET STREET, WARWICK.

Now re-opened with a rare and choice supply of

WINES AND SPIRITS.

Scotch Whiskey (our Speciality),

18s. per Gallon.

HOME BREW'D ALES.

WM. WHYTE, Proprietor.

Wines and Spirits of the best quality, on Draught and in large or small quantities.

BOTTLE AND JUG DEPARTMENT.

Above: *The Millwright Arms, Coten End, Warwick. A short-lived micro-brewery was established here in 1997, in the single-storey building to the right.*

Left: *The Woolpack Hotel in Market Square, Warwick, was a home-brew house in 1873*

THREE

THE RISE AND FALL OF THE COMMON BREWER

The 1830s saw the rise of the common or commercial brewer in Warwickshire. Three of them were established within the decade. Two of the three emerged within a year of each other. Both advertised in the same edition of the *Warwickshire Advertiser* for 11 February 1832. The newspaper records that on 6 February, a public meeting was held at the Swan Hotel in Warwick, which saw the establishment of the Warwick & Leamington Brewery Co. A subscription was launched, with shares of £50 each, in order to raise a working capital of £20,000. The brewery was established in an existing large factory and warehouse, with malthouse, dray house and stabling, measuring some 6,000 square yards. It was situated in Wallace Street, Saltisford, a suburb of Warwick, and would appear to have been Jaggard & Hiorns old worsted mill. The site was purchased for £4,000. A working committee consisting of Dr Jephson, William Collins, Joseph Sanders, Richard Jaggard, William Clarke and Richard Hiorns was installed to run the business. The records of the company have survived and are now housed in the County Record Office. They are an interesting insight into the finance and running of a Common Brewery at this time. The new company costed out their debits and credits, giving them an expected profit of in excess of £3,700 in their first year:

Cost of making one brew	£45 12s 0d
(12 quarters of malt	£40 16s 0d)
(84 lbs hops	£ 4 16s 0d)
Sale of one brew of Ale	
30 barrels at 1s 4d gallon	£72 0s 0d
12 barrels of beer at 3s gallon	£ 5 8s 0d
	£77 8s 0d
Profit on one brew	£31 16s 0d

Assuming 180 brews per year, this would give a profit of £5,724.

Set against this were running costs amounting to £2,000, made up as follows:

	£
Brewer	200
Clerks	300
Stoker & Cooper	100
3 Labourers	100
Draymen	100
Horses	200
Debts	300
Casks	300
Wear & Tear	300

The building, having been purchased, was converted into a brewery, modelled on that of Truman, Hanbury & Buxton of London. George Barnard of Birmingham was brought in as consultant engineer. The brewery was up and running by late 1833.

The other brewery referred to was that of Edward Fordham Flower of Brewery Street, Stratford-upon-Avon. The family had been brewers at Hertford from 1725 to 1818, before migrating to the USA. Returning to England in 1824, Flower eventually established himself at Stratford in 1831. On 11 February 1832 he placed an advert in the *Advertiser,* to promote his business. The brewery grew and expanded, and in 1852 Edward was joined by his son, Charles Flower.

The Warwick Brewery, meanwhile, had undergone a number of changes in its management personnel. In 1852 original partner, Richard Jaggard, retired. By this time the brewery had problems with debt and its water supply. As Flowers, a family-owned and family-run concern, gradually expanded, the committee-run Warwick Brewery began a downward spiral into bankruptcy. In 1864 it went into liquidation. The brewery was sold to Frank Speakman Webb and Percy Barron in 1866, for £4,250. Webb's brother, architect Philip Webb, a friend of William Morris, designed a rather beautiful lozenge-shaped beer label in off-white, black, blue and maroon, part of which was registered as the company's trademark. The label depicts Guy's Tower at Warwick Castle. The new company traded under Barron's name.

The third brewery that came into being during the 1830s was that of Lewis, Haddon & Allenby of Binswood, Leamington. The company was founded in 1839 as ale and porter brewers by Stephen Lewis, a draper, and a Mr Sandeman, who appears to have been a silent partner in the venture. A two-storey tower brewery, powered by a steam engine, was constructed in 1840, to a design by John Tone of Stoneleigh. It included a malthouse, elegant railed walls and an arched entrance in the classical style. Sandeman was soon succeeded by two new partners, John Haddon and Everitt Allenby, Lewis's former partner in the drapery business. By 1860 the brewery was producing seven beers: an IPA, two milds of varying strengths, three different types of stout, and a light, or dinner, ale. Upon his death in 1871, Lewis was succeeded by his son, James Lewis, and the company briefly became Lewis, Haddon & Co. William Wells Ridley, a junior partner who had joined the company in 1868, became a full partner in the business, which became Lewis & Ridley. The new company entered two trademarks: the Warwickshire bear and ragged staff, and its 'sparkling gem' motif.

WARWICK & LEAMINGTON
Brewery Company.

AT A PUBLIC MEETING held at the Swan Hotel, WARWICK, on MONDAY, the 6th Day of FEBRUARY, 1832, pursuant to Advertisement, for establishing a BREWERY, for Making and Supplying the Public with Genuine Porter, Ale, and Beer,

JOHN TOMES, ESQ. M. P. IN THE CHAIR,

THE FOLLOWING RESOLUTIONS

Were severally proposed and carried unanimously :

1st—That a Company be now formed for the purpose of making and supplying the Public with Genuine Porter, Ale, and Beer, to be called "THE WARWICK and LEAMINGTON BREWERY COMPANY."

2d—That a Subscription be now entered into for that purpose, and that the Capital of the Company be £20,000. to be raised in Shares of £50. each. That the Sum of £5. per share be paid on or before the 1st Day of MAY next; and that calls be afterwards made from time to time on the Subscribers as the Committee may see occasion, so that no call exceed the Sum of £5. per share, or be made oftener than once in every month.

3d—That the large Factory, Warehouse, Malthouse, Dray-house, Lofts, Stabling, and about Six Thousand Square Yards of Land, situate in the SALTISFORD, in WARWICK, be purchased at the Sum of £4000. and that the Business of the Company be carried on there.

4th—That a Committee be appointed to carry these Resolutions into effect; and that such Committee consist of the following Gentlemen, viz.—Dr. JEPHSON, Mr. WILLIAM COLLINS, Mr. JOSEPH SANDERS, Mr. RICHARD JAGGARD, Mr. WM. CLARKE, and Mr. RICHARD HIORNS, with power to add to their numbers; and that all Applications for Shares be made to them, or the Solicitor to the Company.

5th—That Messrs, TOMES, TOMES, and RUSSELL be and are hereby appointed Bankers to the Company.

6th—That Mr. S. W. HAYNES be and is hereby appointed the Solicitor to the Company.

Mr. TOMES having left the Chair,

Resolved—That the Thanks of the Meeting be given to Mr. TOMES for his Compliance with the wishes of the Meeting in taking the Chair, and for his Attention to the Business of the Meeting.

By Order of the Committee,

S. W. HAYNES.

The formation of the Warwick & Leamington Brewery Co. was advertised in the Warwickshire Advertiser *on 11 February 1832.*

FLOWER & SONS,

BREWERS, STRATFORD-ON-AVON.

STORES: RUSSELL STREET, LEAMINGTON.

Warwick Office: 44, Brook Street.

Families supplied with Ales & Stout in 9, 18, & 36 Gallon Casks.

H. P. GIBBONS, Manager.

An early advertisement for Flowers Brewery, Stratford-upon-Avon.

The beautiful bottle label of Webb & Barron's Warwick Brewery Co., designed by architect Philip Webb around 1866. It depicts Guy's Tower at Warwick Castle.

At Stratford-upon-Avon in 1870, Flowers opened a new brewery on Birmingham Road. An illustration and description of it appeared in the *Illustrated Midland News* for 22 January 1870. The company by that date was employing some 150 men in production and distribution, and 45 clerks and commercial travellers. They had established regional offices in London, Birmingham, Bristol, Cheltenham and Leamington. After describing the layout of the new brewery, with additional maltings built alongside the railway line, the reporter described the advancements that Flowers had made. Over a period of some four years they had experimented with beer cooling, spending upwards of £2,000 in the purchase of one of Kirk's ice-making machines. By experimentation they successfully sidestepped the ice-making process and applied the chillers to the direct cooling of the beer. Where Flowers led, the other big brewers followed. As to production, by 1870 Flowers Brewery had almost 40,000 casks in use. A curious little story relating to Flowers casks appeared in the magazine *Punch* on 29 April 1865. The company had taken Cheltenham brewers Pole's to court over using their casks. While there was no suggestion of fraud intended – in other words, trying to sell Pole's beer as Flowers – the Stratford company sued that Pole's had soured the barrels by using them. The *Cheltenham Examiner* reported the case:

> *During the progress of the trial, MR TAYTON produced a sample of the beer, in a tumbler, which being, as he alleged, acid, tended, according to his argument, to injure the casks. The foreman of the jury, to whom it was handed, in order to test its quality, tasted it, smacked his lips, and drank it off at a draught – much to the astonishment and indignation of the worthy Under Sheriff – who spoke in terms of complaint to the offender. The foreman excused himself by saying that he 'was rather thirsty'. As may be imagined, this way of sifting evidence created much amusement in Court.*

Lewis, Haddon & Allenby's Leamington Brewery, 1846.

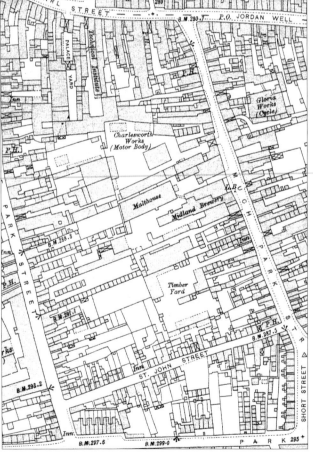

Brewers.

MARRIOTT & SON, the
Midland brewery, Much
park street
Ratliff, Wm., the Coventry Brewery,
leicester row

Top left: *Flowers Brewery, Stratford-upon-Avon, 1870.*

Top right: *The Flowers trademark, registered in 1877.*

Above: *Marriott & Son's Midland Brewery, Coventry.*

Left: *A nineteenth-century map showing the Midland Brewery in Much Park Street, Coventry.*

Such an action rather destroyed Flowers' case. While the jury found in their favour, it awarded them just one farthing in damages.

In 1877, Frank Phillips and W.H. Marriott took over the old Midland Brewery of James Marriott & Son in Much Park Street, Coventry. The original firm had been founded some three years after Flowers' farcical court case, in 1868. Frank Phillips was the driving force behind the new company. The old brewery had just three tied houses within the city, but were considerable suppliers to the free trade. As other breweries began expanding their tied-house stables, inevitably encroaching upon the company's free trade outlets, Phillips & Marriott began an active policy of buying up these houses. In 1900 they registered as a limited liability company in order to raise money to take over local rivals Ratcliff's Coventry Brewery of Leicester Road. This was the old Summerfield, Lloyd & Owen Brewery, founded in 1801, the oldest surviving brewery within the county. Following its successful takeover, the Midland Brewery increased its stable of tied houses from twenty-nine to sixty-three, in and around the city. The Midland Brewery at this date was employing a staff of sixty to run its brewery, which had nine fermenting vessels. At any one time there were 10,000 casks in circulation. Phillips, who had been appointed managing director of the new company, died less than a year later, in February 1901. For a number of years after this, lacking Phillips' drive, the company went into decline, before bouncing back in 1904. They opened additional premises at Rugby and Atherstone that year, and in 1908 commissioned a new brewery alongside their old premises in Much Park Street. This state-of-the-art brewery was designed by London brewing architects William Bradford & Sons of Regent Street. The new construction was a 30-quarter brewery built in red brick with stone dressings, and was six and a half storeys high. It consisted of a boiler house, copper house, brew house, fermenting house and racking room. Additional cellars were built beneath the new building, linking up to the old brewery cellars. The new brewery was constructed by Dennett & Ingle and opened in June 1909. In the period after the First World War, the brewery went into decline once more. Tied houses were sold off to raise money. Competition grew fierce. In April 1924 Phillips & Marriott was taken over by Bass. Later that year the brewery was closed down. During the terrible Blitz on Coventry during the Second World War, the building was badly damaged. It was finally demolished in 1971.

The Alcester Brewery Co. was established by George Henry Heap Haines in Church Street, Alcester, in 1886. It was not destined to become one of the big county brewers, and is typical of many other second-division breweries like Zephaniah Brown's Fenny Compton Brewery or Thomas Dewis' Bedworth Brewery. Expansion was cautious and in time it established a modest stable of eighteen tied houses. In 1889 Haines felt confident enough to go public and registered the brewery as a company. The following year Lionel James was appointed manager. In partnership with Edward J. Neale, he bought out Haines. Confident of their ability, they were brought up sharp by competition from the likes of near neighbours Flowers of Stratford, who had begun an aggressive policy of expansion. In September 1899 the Alcester Brewery was put up for auction. The sales catalogue also gives details of their tied houses:

Alcester	*The Royal Oak, The New Inn, The Talbot Inn and The Bakers' Arms.*
Studley	*The Hog in the Hole, The Black Horse, The Bricklayers' Arms, The Griffin Inn and a beerhouse in Littlewood Green.*
Redditch	*The Village Inn, Beoley; The Oddfellows' Arms, Astwood Bank; The Britannia, The Golden Lion, The Red Lion.*
Others	*The Fish Hotel, Wixford; The Orange Tree, Knowle; The White Swan, Stratford-upon-Avon; The Hop Pole, Birmingham; and The Drainers' Arms, Himbleton.*

Failing to reach the reserve of £16,000, the brewery was withdrawn from sale. The outlying houses were either sold or leased in separate deals. The company struggled on with increasing debts until 1911, when the receiver was called in. Assets were sold off to meet debts and the streamlined company continued brewing until 1914. Thereafter it turned to bottling other breweries' beer, finally closing around 1924.

As new breweries emerged and others were taken over, Barron's Warwickshire Brewery was acquired by Dutton & Sons of Witney, Oxfordshire, for £16,500. The partners had succeeded in turning the business around and at its sale to Dutton & Sons in 1879, Warwickshire Brewery had twelve tied houses and was producing 9,050 barrels of beer a year. The new company traded as Dutton & Hudson until 1896, when the company and its 128 tied houses were taken over by Morton Lucas, Percy Allan Leaf and Gordon Lyon Bland, trading as Lucas & Co. This company had taken over Lewis & Ridley's Leamington Brewery in 1885, along with their thirty-five tied houses, for £75,000. In July 1897, Lucas & Co. registered as a limited liability company in order to take over the business of the same name. In 1928 Lucas & Co. took over Lucas, Blackwell & Arkwright's Brewery in Warwick Street, Rugby, along with their 124 tied houses. Covetous eyes were watching and later that year Ansell's Brewery of Birmingham took them over. The brewery was closed in 1934.

The last of the big Warwickshire breweries was that of H.E. Thornley Ltd of Radford Semele, Leamington Spa. It was 1899 before they were established, quite late by most standards. Architecturally the building was impressive. It was four storeys high, with a central seven-storey-high castellated tower. The Radford Hall Brewery was constructed in a Gothic-baronial style, in red brick with a line of yellow brick coursing at each storey. Expansion went on apace. Hostile takeover bids were rejected and Thornley's gained a reputation for independence. By 1920, in addition to draught ale, the brewery was producing four bottled ales: Sunbright Ale, Nourishing Stout – both of which were awarded gold medals – a light Dinner Ale and a Family Ale, which was awarded a gold medal in London that same year. The company also expanded into the wine and spirit trade. In 1933 the company finally agreed to a merger with Birmingham-based Benjamin Kelsey Ltd, to form Thornley Kelsey Ltd. The company was later renamed Benjamin Kelsey Ltd. The brewery, apparently in financial difficulties and certainly facing keen competition not only from Flowers but also from Ansell's and M&B, closed in October 1968 to concentrate on its wholesale wine business. Its twenty-two tied houses were sold off, the majority being bought up by Davenport's, Birmingham's third big brewer. Thornley's main brewery block was later demolished.

Flowers meanwhile had expanded production. By 1888 they were producing thirteen different beers: IPA, Light Pale, Bitter, three Strong Ales, two Milds, three Family Ales, an Extra Stout and a Porter. The bitter, also known as Guinea Ale, was recommended for 'the use of invalids'. Later, their beers, including Brown Ale, were also bottled by outside distributors, including G.F. & A. Brown of Wrexham. The company was also involved in a series of takeovers in a bid to increase their stable of tied houses. Flowers acquired the Caudle Well Brewery of Shipston-on-Stour in 1896. Three years later they acquired the Tavistock Brewery Co. of Tavistock, Devon, giving them access to the West Country. Closer to home, they gobbled up the little Gardner Brothers Brewery at Little Compton in Warwickshire and Gillett's Swan Brewery of Moreton-in-Marsh, Gloucestershire, in 1900. In the period after the First World War, they bought up Fortescue & Son of Bromsgrove, Worcestershire, in 1926, and Rowland's Brewery of Evesham in 1948. At the outbreak of the Second World War, with 350 tied houses Flowers had become the largest brewery company in Warwickshire, excluding Birmingham.

In the post-war period, Flowers introduced four new brews: Dragon's Blood, a barley wine which was awarded the Grand Prix at Brussels, Prague and Pilsen; Brewmaster, a pale ale, with the recommendation that it be served chilled; Poacher, a strong, full smooth brown ale; and a strong German lager. The company started to rebuild at Stratford but during this period the quality of their beer became variable. Complaints began to endanger their long-established reputation. In 1954 an amalgamation was negotiated with the brewers J.W. Green of Luton, Bedfordshire. The new grouping was renamed Flowers Breweries Ltd, the name J.W. Green not being generally known outside Bedfordshire. The new company controlled nearly 1,500 tied houses. The problems at Stratford were sorted out, being mainly due to poor drainage, and Flowers' reputation was restored. In 1962 the company was taken over by Whitbread & Co. of London. Flowers Phoenix Brewery at Luton, and that at Stratford, were closed in 1969. Warwickshire was left without a single common brewer.

The Alcester Brewery.

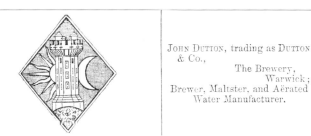

Dutton & Co.'s registered trademark for the Warwick Brewery.

Lucas, Blackwell & Arkwright's Leamington Brewery

DUTTON & CO.,
THE BREWERY,
WARWICK.

LIST OF PRICES.
(DELIVERED).

	MARK.	HOGSHEAD. £ s. d.	BARREL. £ s. d.	KILDERKIN. £ s. d.	FIRKIN. s. d.
East India Pale Ale	I.P.A.	4 1 0	2 14 0	1 7 0	13 6
Guinea Ale - - -	No. 6.	3 3 0	2 2 0	1 1 0	10 6
Light Bitter Ale -	B.A.	2 14 0	1 16 0	0 18 0	9 0
[Brewed expressly for Family use].					
Very Strong Ale -	XXXX.	4 10 0	3 0 0	1 10 0	15 0
Strong Ale - - -	BXXX.	4 1 0	2 14 0	1 7 0	13 6
Mild Dinner Ale -	No. 5.	3 12 0	2 8 0	1 4 0	12 0
Do. -	XX.	2 14 0	1 16 0	0 18 0	9 0
Do. -	X.	2 0 6	1 7 0	0 13 6	6 9
Table Beer - - -	T.	1 7 0	0 18 0	0 9 0	4 6
Double Brown Stout	D.B.S.	4 1 0	2 14 0	1 7 0	13 6
Double Stout - -	D.S.	3 12 0	2 8 0	1 4 0	12 0

These ALES AND STOUTS are brewed with water of first class brewing properties (analysis by E. R. SOUTHBY, ESQ., F.C.S.) and choice Malt and Hops, and are GUARANTEED PURE.

They are brilliant, sparkling, and particularly easy of digestion.

The EAST INDIA PALE ALE (I.P.A.) will bear comparison with the finest Burton Ales ; and the LIGHT BITTER ALE (B.A.) which is brewed expressly for Family use, is a special ale, combining the advantages of the best German beers with a delicious flavour and aroma which cannot be surpassed.

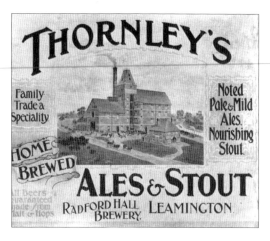

Top left: *Dutton & Co.'s price list, 1890.*

Top right: *Flowers' beer, bottled in Wrexham.*

Below left: *Thornley's Radford Hall Brewery, Leamington.*

Below right: *The post-war range of Flowers beers.*

1 DRAGON'S BLOOD

A strong Old English ale generally known as a Barley Wine, this is the strongest of our beers. It has achieved the unique distinction of being awarded the Grand Prix at Brussels, Prague and Pilsen. It is available in nip bottles as well as small bottles.

2 BREWMASTER

A superb Pale Ale specially brewed to give a deliciously full, but clean flavour. This has become one of the country's outstanding bottled beers. It is particularly recommended for home entertaining. Serve slightly chilled. The nip size bottle is a special favourite amongst women.

3 LAGER

A really high-quality lager beer of the stronger German type. It should, of course, be served chilled to bring out the fine, smooth flavour.

4 POACHER

A full, smooth, brown beer for those who prefer a softer but stronger type of brown ale. Keep some at home for the younger members of the family and their friends.

5 LIGHT ALE

A clean-tasting ale, fine to drink with food. Slightly chilled there is no more refreshing drink. Special Golding hops give this beer the wonderfully delicate flavour that won it 1st Prize, Silver Medal, and Diploma at the Brewers' Exhibition, London 1934.

6 NUT BROWN ALE

A clean-drinking ale with a drier palate than Poacher. A first-class brown ale to drink with your meal. It's available in large and small bottles.

The accompanying tasting notes for the Flowers beers.

FLOWER & SONS, LIMITED,

India Pale Ale Brewers,

STRATFORD-ON-AVON.

LEAMINGTON STORES: RUSSELL STREET.

We beg to call attention to our **INDIA PALE ALE,** Light Pale and Bitter Beer or Guinea Ale, which we recommend particularly for **THE USE OF INVALIDS;** also to our **XK** and **AK FAMILY ALES.** These are brewed from the **BEST MALT AND HOPS ONLY,** are pale in colour and delicate in flavour, and guaranteed to be absolutely pure. *See annexed Copy of County Analyst's Report :*

[COPY.]
County Analyst's Laboratory,
Unity Buildings, Temple Street, Birmingham,
October 7th, 1887.

I hereby certify that I have analysed samples of Messrs. Flower & Sons' Ales and found them perfectly pure, wholesome, and remarkably free from Acidity or any injurious substance.

I am of opinion that they are of excellent quality.

(Signed) A. BOSTOCK HILL, M.D., F.I.C.
Public Analyst to the County of Warwick, &c., &c.

Prices—Delivered by Dray.

	36 Galls.	18 Galls.	9 Galls.
India Pale Ale	60/-	30/-	15/-
Light Pale	48/-	24/-	12/-
Bitter Beer	42/-	21/-	10/6
Strong Ale, No. 1	72/-	36/-	18/-
do. No. 2	60/-	30/-	15/-
do. No. 3	54/-	27/-	13/6
Mild Ale, XXX	48/-	24/-	12/-
do. XX	42/-	21/-	10/6
Family Ale, XK	36/-	18/-	9/-
do. AK	30/-	15/-	7/6
do. A	24/-	12/-	6/-
Extra Stout	48/-	24/-	12/-
Porter	36/-	18/-	9/-

DISCOUNT ALLOWED FOR CASH.

N.B.—The Light Pale Ale, Double Stout, and XK Family Ale supplied also in 4½ Gall. Casks if required.

Flowers Brewery price list, 1890.

FOUR

MODERNITY AND MICRO-BREWERIES

There are, alas, no major breweries remaining in Warwickshire. However, this does not mean that brewing has ceased – far from it. As breweries closed down across the country, a new breed of small brewery, the micro-brewery, started up. In Warwickshire the first of these was the Studley Brewery, perhaps better known as Washford Mill Brewery. It was established in September 1978 by Michael Cannon. The old needle-making mill was converted into a pub and restaurant. The beer was brewed in an outbuilding behind The new brewery was an instant success, especially with drinkers from south Birmingham, bored with the duopoly of Ansell's and M&B. Studley Brewery produced three excellent beers – Old Glory, Studley Bitter and Studley Giant – and you could enjoy them on a warm summer's evening in the beer garden, as you watched the hedge-clipping antics of the F111 fighter-bombers training in low level flight overhead. Set in the countryside, the brewery was subject to wild yeast infection, and this was to prove its undoing. Failure to control the infection led to variations in the taste of its beers and a falling-off in custom. Brewing finally ceased here in October 1982.

Where Studley led, others followed. In May 1992 Graham Judge opened a micro-brewery at Church Lawford. He began by producing two beers. With demand assured, Judge moved to a 10-barrel plant in Rugby. Following a slight hiccup in April 1999, when the brewery temporarily closed, it re-emerged two months later as Judge's Real Ale Brewery. There were financial problems though and, when the lease fell due, the brewery closed with the intention of relocating. It never happened. As such, it was a lesson to others. In 1994 Stewart Elliott established a 4-barrel plant in an old stable block at Church End, Shustoke. It was a bit of a struggle but it succeeded. In September 2000 the brewery moved to a 10-barrel plant in Ridge Lane, Atherstone. Church End Brewery has just under 150 outlets and produces a staggering 30 different beers a year. Beers include Poacher's Pocket, a good session beer at 3.5%; Vicar's Ruin (4.4%); and Fallen Angel (5.1%).

Old Washford Mill

The HOME of STUDLEY BREWERY
"Old Glory" and "Studley Bitter"

See it brewed on the premises, using an original recipe of 1741.
See the old brewing methods in our Brewery Museum.
Lunchtime Hot and Cold Buffets Monday to Friday.

ICKNIELD STREET DRIVE, STUDLEY, WARWICKSHIRE
Telephone: (0527) 23068

Left: Studley Brewery, Washford Mill, 1980.

Below: Church End Brewery, formerly of Shustoke, now of Nuneaton.

Warwickshire Brewery Ltd was opened in December 1995 by Philip Page, at Princes Drive, Kenilworth. It closed in December 1997 and that appeared to be that. But Page had merely relocated. In November 1998 the company reappeared as the Warwickshire Beer Co. in Queen's Street, Cubbington, near Leamington. They began by producing six barrels a week. This had expanded to twenty-six by the year 2000. In May 2001 the company bought up the Market Tavern as its principal outlet, but in addition it also acquired a further eighty free-trade outlets. Most people can brew a half-decent beer, but the trick is selling it. This is what Page achieved. The Warwickshire Beer Co. brew Best Bitter (ABV 3.9%), Lady Godiva (4.2%), St Patrick's (4.4%), Flagstaff (4.4%), Castle (4.6%), Golden Beer (4.9%) and Kingmaker (5.5%). The brewery also produce a bottled beer, Old Warwick, which is available in local Tesco supermarkets.

Some micro-breweries were not so successful. A small brewery at the Bull's Head in Alcester produced a limited number of brews in 1996 but then closed. Fat God's Brewery, a silly name but one that stood out, was established at the Queen's Head in Iron Cross, near Evesham, by Andrew Miller. It opened in the summer of 1997. Like Page, Miller knew that he had to secure free-trade outlets, and this he attempted to do. The brewery produced fourteen different beers and received active support from the local CAMRA branches, who seemed to feature it in every one of their publications over the next four years. However, the business closed in December 2001. Likewise the micro-brewery established at the rear of the Millwright Arms at Coten End, Warwick, in December 1997 was forced to close in the summer of 1998, upon the instructions of the pub's owners, Punch Taverns. Also in 1997, the Feldon Brewery at the Coach & Horses, New Street, Shipston-on-Stour, was forced to close for renovation and extensions to the pub. Unfortunately the new plans did not include a new micro-brewery.

Cox's Brewery was established in a moment of enlightenment by the Charles Wells Brewery of Bedford. It was opened at the old Cox's timber yard, down by the river at Stratford, in 1998. To the delight of the women's movement, its first two brewers were women: Sarah-Jane Anderson and Anna Davis. Its third and last brewer was John Pilling. Amid unconvincing arguments, Wells pulled the plug on the brewery in January 2000.

The Frankton Bagby Brewery was established at the Old Stables, Church Lawford, Rugby. It opened in April 1999 and, with 150 free-trade outlets, its future looks secure. It produces six standard beers: Peeping Tom (3.8%), Old Chestnut (4.0%), Chicken Tackle (4.1%), Squires Brew (4.2%), Top Tipple (4.2%), and Rugby Special (4.5%). The brewery also produce a winter special, Christmas Pudding (7.0%). This is a very dark beer which smells and tastes like Christmas pudding. Also established in the spring of 1999 was the North Cotswold Brewery of David Tilbrook. It is situated near Shipston-on-Stour. Its postal address is Moreton-in-Marsh, Gloucestershire, but the brewery itself does lie just within the Warwickshire border. It is a 10-barrel plant, supplying the Black Horse Inn at Shipston and over forty other outlets.

In 2003 three new micro-breweries were established in Warwickshire: the Wizard Brewery at Whichford, near Shipston-on-Stour; the Slaughterhouse Brewery, Emscote, Warwick; and Walsh's Bakehouse Brewery, also at Warwick. The Wizard Brewery, established by Mike and Carole Garner, is situated in a barn behind the Norman Knight pub. Its first brew was sold on 27 March 2003. Wizard began with a 1.25-barrel plant, purchased from Swaled Ale Brewery in Gunnerside, North Yorkshire, but have expanded to a 5-barrel plant to cope with demand. Available as regulars in the Norman Knight are Apprentice (ABV 3.6%), One for the Toad (4%) and Druids Fluid (5%). In addition, they produce six seasonal beers. In the summer of 2004 Wizard supplied beer to the Great British Beer Festival at Olympia. The following summer, 2005, the brewery won three best-of-show beers at Warwickshire festivals. Just over the border in Oxfordshire, Druids Fluid was voted best beer at the Hook Norton Beer Festival in July 2005. So confident are they that they are even selling Wizard Brewery polo shirts.

The Slaughterhouse Brewery at Bridge Street in Emscote, Warwick, opened in the summer of 2003, using the old 4-barrel plant from the Church End Brewery. By 2005 they had twenty outlets, including the nearby Simple Simon at Emscote and the exotic Globe Hotel in Theatre Street, Warwick. Beers by Slaughterhouse include Swillmore Original (4.2%), Swillmore Pale Ale (4.5%) and Wild Boar (5%).

Walsh's, who share a site with Margaret Hall Bakery in Miller's Road, Warwick, was started up in June 2003 by husband and wife team Jonathan and Charlotte Walsh. Charlotte, as at the summer of 2005, is the only woman brewer in Warwickshire. The company began with a flying start when their 4.4% Flying Top Ale was voted best beer of the Harbury Beer Festival. This is a rich amber ale with a floral aroma. The brewery uses a 5-barrel plant from the old Firkin brew house in Reading. In addition, the brewery produces Bakehouse Bitter (3.8%), described as a session bitter, and Old Gridlap (5.0%), a rich dark copper-coloured strong ale. Outlets include the CAMRA-listed Old Fourpenny Shop in Crompton Street, Warwick; the Little Lark in Studley (formerly a Mad O'Rourke's pub); the Holly Bush, Alcester; and the highly recommended Case is Altered at Five Ways, Hatton, a gem of an untouched pub.

In the autumn of 2004, the Fantasy Brewery was launched. Based at the rear of Lloyd's Free House in Bond Street, Nuneaton, its first brew went on sale in October. The brewery is run by pub licensees Bob and Pam Tweedle. The brewery plant came from the Rat & Ratchet in Huddersfield. There are three beers as regulars: Slurp & Burp, a pale hoppy beer (ABV 4.3%); Dragon's Bane, a wheat beer (4.3%); and Woblin' Goblin, a dark fruity beer (4.6%).

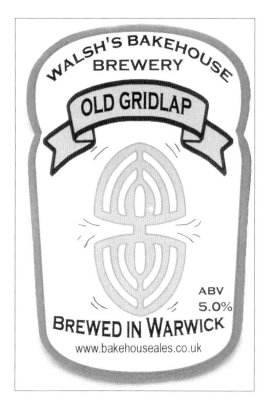

Opposite page: *Slaughterhouse Brewery, Bridge Street, Warwick.*

This page: *Pump handle motifs for Walsh's Bakehouse Brewery, Millers Road, Warwick.*

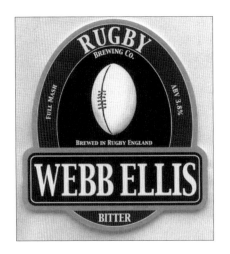

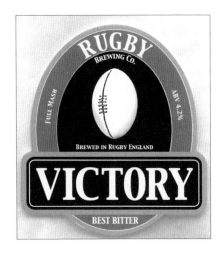

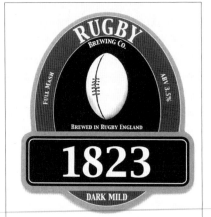

Rugby Brewing Co. pump handle motifs.

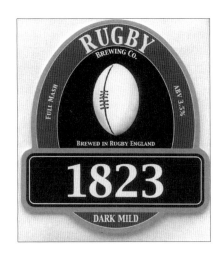

In late November 2004 came news of the establishment of yet another Warwickshire brewery. The Purity Brewery of Spernall Ash, near Studley, is intended to be a 20-barrel plant with a visitors' centre in which will be sold the company's bottled ales. The Purity Brewery has been started by Paul Halsey, formerly of the Highgate Brewery in Walsall, and his business partner James Minkin. Two beers have been identified for production, a light session beer at 3.9% and an organic premium ale at 4.4%. The company intend to produce their own organic barley for greater control over their product. Their first brew was available in December 2005.

Around the same time came news of another new micro-brewery, the Rugby Brewery Co., established on an industrial estate on the edge of the town by Steve Miller. Its main brew, Webb Ellis, went on to win the silver medal at the Rugby Beer Festival in 2005. At 3.8% ABV, it is an ideal session beer. The brewery, on the Somers Road industrial estate, is capable of producing 288 gallons of beer at a time and has three main outlets: the Imperial Hotel in Oxford Street, the Red Lion in Hillmorton and the White Room nightclub in Railway Terrace. In the town that gave birth to rugby football, their beers all have a rugby connection and it is the intention of the company to capitalise on this by seeking out further outlets with rugby clubs across the country. So far the response has been favourable. Other beers produced by the Rugby Brewing Co. include 1823 Dark Mild (ABV 3.5%), which is very smooth with a roasted malt finish; Victory Best Bitter (4.2%), described as a 'classic best bitter'; Union Premium Ale (4.4%), a strong pale ale which is ideal as a summer drink; and No.8 Strong Ale (5.0%), a more full-bodied darker beer. In addition, the company also brew what they describe as an 'English lager' called Penalty, with an ABV of 4.0%.

In the spring of 2005 came news of the establishment of yet another micro-brewery, the Atomic Brewery, based at the Alexandra Arms in James Street, Rugby. Brewing began in earnest in December 2005. Behind the Lord Nelson, along Birmingham Road, Pete Ansley, Bob Yates and Mike Walsh established their Tunnel Brewery. Their initial beer was Late Ott, available in the Lord Nelson. Though not directly associated with the brewery, the Nelson has shown tremendous support, even allocating two pumps to the young brewery's ales. It is the sort of thing that raises the happiness levels of beer drinkers everywhere. Will all these new breweries survive? It's up to you. Drink more Warwickshire beer – and drink it often!

ALCESTER,

Warwickshire.

PARTICULARS, PLAN & CONDITIONS OF SALE

OF

The Alcester Brewery

Close to Alcester Station in connection with the Midland and Gt. Western
Railways, seven miles from Redditch and eleven from Evesham,

FITTED WITH EXCELLENT

EIGHT=QUARTER STEAM PLANT,

AND COMPRISING

Retail Wine and Spirit Business, Clerks' Offices, convenient Residence,
Cellars, Spacious Yard, Stabling, Stores, exceptionally fine BOWLING
GREEN, Gardens and Grounds running down to the River Arrow.

A SIX=QUARTER BRICK=BUILT MALTING,

Held upon Lease, and

EIGHTEEN PUBLIC & BEER HOUSES

(Several of which are of **Freehold Tenure**),

COTTAGES & OTHER PROPERTY.

The Sales which have steadily increased during the last few years now amount to about

£7,000 Per Annum,

And the whole will be offered by Auction, in One Lot (unless previously disposed of
privately), by Messrs.

BARKER & NEALE

At the Mart, Tokenhouse Yard, London, E.C.,

On WEDNESDAY, 6th SEPTEMBER, 1899,

At TWO o'clock precisely.

Particulars, Plan and Conditions of Sale may be obtained of W. S. TUNBRIDGE, Esq., Solicitor, Redditch ;
and of the Auctioneers,

13, Lowndes Street, London, S.W.

The Alcester Brewery sales particulars, 1899.

A LIST OF WARWICKSHIRE BREWERIES

ALCESTER BREWERY LTD, Church Street.
Established in 1886, the directors comprised George Henry Heap Haines and his son. They registered as a company in September 1889. This four-storey brewery, with a frontage of 43ft onto Church Street, was an 8-quarter steam brewery with maltings in Henley Street, behind the Bakers Arms. Lionel James was appointed manager in the following year. With partner Edward J. Neale, Lionel James took over the firm. Neale took on the role as manager of the business on a day to-day basis. Failing in the face of stern competition, the company and its assets were offered for auction on 6 September 1899, along with its eighteen tied houses. Failing to meet its reserve of £16,000, it was withdrawn. The company continued to brew until February 1911, with Robert Meatyard as manager. On 21 February 1911, the receiver was called in and the company was run by him until 1914. Thereafter it became a beer bottling plant until around 1924.

ATKINS & BOSLEY, Clarendon Brewery, 59 Clarendon Street, Leamington Spa.
Brewing from 1915 to 1919. Thereafter they closed down the brewery to concentrate on their wine and spirit trade.

RICHARD AVERY, Alcester. Listed as a common brewer in 1845.

J. W. BAKER, Castle Brewery, Leamington Spa.
In existence by 1846, they do not appear to have had any tied houses but seem to have supplied the free trade. Advertising in *William's Directory Advertiser*, they announced 'The usual discount for Hotel and Innkeepers'. Baker's were ale and porter brewers, also brewing East India Pale Ale and Fine Old Ale. XXX ale was sold to the trade at 1s 8d a gallon, as was their XXXP Porter.

ZEPHANIAH M. BROWN, Fenny Compton Brewery, 41 George Street, Fenny Compton, and Banbury.

Established by Richard Guest Brown, a former coal merchant, in 1875. The George & Dragon pub at Fenny Compton Wharf acted as the brewery tap. In 1892 the business was taken over by Zephaniah Matthew Brown. In January 1897 the business was registered as Zeph. M. Brown & Co. Ltd and took over Richard William Flick's Horse Shoe Brewery in Parson Street, Banbury. Possibly because he had overreached himself financially, Brown closed down the Fenny Compton brewery and moved production to Banbury. The Fenny Compton site was turned into a store and was in use up to 1903. On 19 January 1898 Brown was declared bankrupt, with debts of £3,424. The receiver stepped in but, failing to find a buyer, the firm was wound up in 1906.

CAUDLEWELL BREWERY

See William Turner.

JOHN CAVE, Royal Oak Brewery, Brandon, and at the Rose & Crown, Brook Lane, Wolston. John Cave, the son of Mrs Sarah Cave who was listed as a retail brewer herself in 1854, had by 1866 secured the licence of the Royal Oak in Brandon. Two years later he was also listed as a brewer and maltster. By 1880 Cave was also licensee of the nearby Rose & Crown in Wolston, just across the river. In *White's History, Gazetteer & Directory* for 1874, Cave is listed as 'victualler, brewer, wine & spirit merchant and agent for Burton Ales and Dublin stout, Royal Oak Inn, and collector of rates and taxes for the last 20 years'. Cave died in 1904. The Brandon brewery closed in 1906, though brewing continued under his executors at the Rose & Crown up to 1921. The business was then taken over by Elijah Strong.

JOHN CAVE,
BREWER,
BRANDON AND WOLSTON

AGENTS —MR. R. L. FLANDERS, 13, Weston Street.
MR. H. J. PALMER, 2, Trafalgar Street.

Ales Pure and Full to the Bung.

Cave's Brewery, Wolston.

CHURCH END BREWERY,

Shustoke.

This 4-barrel plant was opened in a 350-year-old stable block next to the Griffin Inn by Stewart Elliot in 1994. It moved to a 10-barrel plant at Ridge Lane, Atherstone, in September 2000. It now supplies some 100 free-trade outlets with over 30 different beers, including Gravediggers, a very dark mild with a suggestion of chocolate in the aftertaste (ABV 3.8%); Without-a-bix, a wheat beer (ABV 4.2%); and Vicar's Ruin, a best bitter (ABV 4.4%).

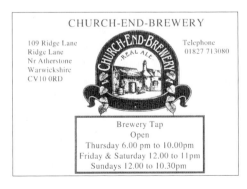

An advertisement for the Church End Brewery.

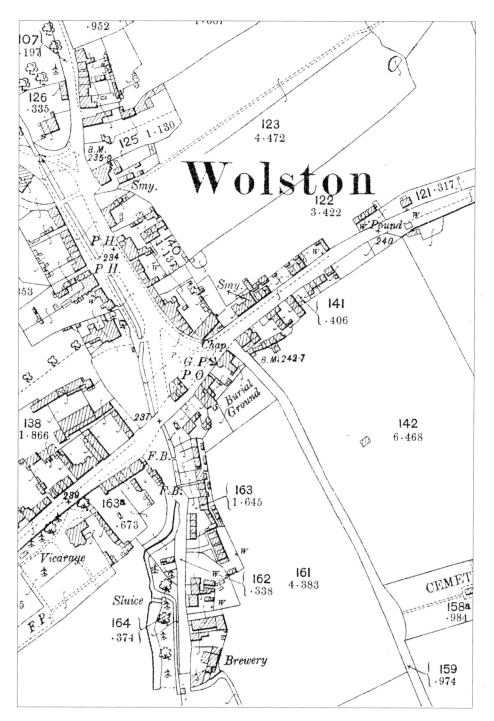

A late nineteenth-century map showing Cave's Brewery at the southern end of Wolston village, near Coventry.

CITY MALTINGS, Cox Street, Coventry.
Additional premises of Atkinson's of Aston, Birmingham. Listed as brewers in *Kelly's Directory of Warwickshire* for 1892. Brewing does appear to have taken place here.

CLARENDON BREWERY, 59 Clarendon Street, Leamington Spa.
Run by Atkins & Bosley between 1915-19. It later stopped brewing to concentrate on its wine and spirit trade.

THOMAS CLARIDGE, 13 Cook Street, Coventry.
Listed as a common brewer from 1914-36. No tied houses known; he appears to have been supplying the free trade.

COVENTRY BREWERY CO.
See William Ratcliff, Joseph Phillips & Son and Summerfield, Lloyd & Co.

THOMAS COX & CO., Market Place, Tamworth.
Wine and spirit merchant and common brewer, 1845.

COX'S YARD BREWERY, Stratford-upon-Avon.
Established in 1998 by Charles Wells' Brewery of Bedford, in a former timber yard near the river Avon. A 5-barrel plant was installed. The brewery had three brewers in its short life, the first two being women, Sarah-Jane Anderson and Anna Davis. In January 2002 Wells' closed down the brewery, terminating the contract of Cox's Yard's third brewer, John Pilling. A special brew was permitted for an agreed beer festival at the brewery tap in May 2002. The plant was put up for sale at £30,000, including removal and transfer to anywhere in mainland UK.

DABBS & NICHOLSON, Coleshill Brewery (and at Great Haywood, Staffs.).
In existence by 1920 as Dabbs Brewery Ltd, with George Moorhouse as manager. He was succeeded by Joseph Moseley in 1926. The company became Dabbs & Nicholson in 1931. The brewery closed in 1936.

THOMAS DEWIS & CO., Rye Piece, King Street, Bedworth.
The company was established in 1893 and remained in the family until the death of Thomas Dewis in August 1905. The King's Head in King Street acted as the brewery tap. The company also sold to the free trade, Enoch Richards being the brewery's agent. Following Dewis' death, the company was placed in the hands of the executors. The old brewery was apparently demolished, or extensively redeveloped, and a new brewery was constructed. It was known as the Lion Brewery. In September 1913 the brewery was put up for auction and purchased by Thomas Daniels. The company later became Randle & Daniels, and later the Bedworth Brewery Co. It operated from 1921-24. The brewery, having closed, was later converted into the St Francis of Assisi Roman Catholic Social Club.

DUTTON & HUDSON, Warwick Brewery, 4 Swan Street, Warwick.
The Warwick & Leamington Brewery Co. was founded in February 1832 at Wallace Street, Warwick. Richard Hiorns was appointed manager in 1834, whereafter the company traded as Jaggard, Hiorns & Collins. In 1835 it became Jaggard & Hiorns, being Richard Jaggard and

Atkinsons Brewery

Limited.

TRADE  MARK

REGISTERED.

Aston Park Brewery, BIRMINGHAM,

And COX STREET, COVENTRY.

TELEPHONE—BIRMINGHAM **260** EAST.   COVENTRY **21.**

FINEST

Ales, Wines, and Spirits.

ALES IN CASK.

					Pin. [4½-gallons].	Firkin. [9-gallons].	Kilderkin. [18-gallons].
XX	Fine Dinner Ale	...	...		4/6	9 -	18/–
XXX	Mild Ale	...	...	...	6/-	12/–	24 -
XXXXX	Old Strong Ale	...	...		9/-	18/–	36/-
A.K.	Light Bitter Ale				4/6	9/–	18 -
F.A.	Family Pale Ale	...	...		4/6	9 -	18/–
P.A.	Superior Pale Ale	...	...		6 -	12/ -	24/-
I.P.A.	India Pale Ale	...	...		6/9	13 6	27 -

OUR SPECIALITIES :

# THAT'LL DO	# WHY NOT
Scotch WHISKY.	Irish WHISKEY.
Guaranteed 10 years old.	Guaranteed 10 years old.
3 4 per bottle.	**3 4** per bottle.

City Maltings, Cox Street, Coventry.

Richard Hiorns. Jaggard took over the management of the company following Hiorns' death in 1845. Briefly the company was Jaggard & Jaggard, before Hiorns' son John joined the board. Richard Jaggard retired in 1852 and new partner Benjamin Russell replaced him. He in turn was replaced by brewer J.H. Marriott. In 1864 the company went into liquidation. It was purchased by Frank Speakman Webb and Percy Barron (*see* Webb and Barron). In 1879 Jonas Paston, acting on behalf of Dutton & Sons of Witney, Oxfordshire, purchased the brewery for £16,500. At the time, it had twelve tied houses and was producing 9,050 barrels a year. The firm traded as Dutton & Hudson from 1888-96. In 1888 the firm acquired further premises at 50 Clarendon Avenue, Leamington Spa. By 1892 they had established offices at Birmingham, Rugby and Solihull. The brewery was acquired by Lucas & Co. of Leamington Spa, along with its 12 tied houses, in 1896. Brewing continued up to 1928.

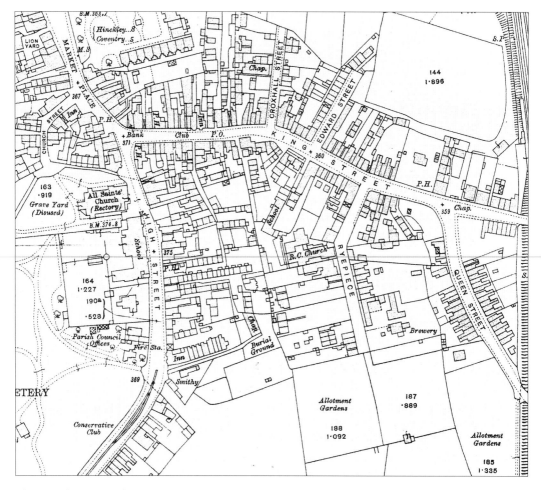

Above: *A late nineteenth-century map showing Dewis' Brewery, Rye Piece, Bedworth.*

Opposite: *An 1890 price list for Dutton & Hudson's Brewery, Warwick.*

DUTTON & HUDSON,

THE BREWERY,

WARWICK.

LIST OF PRICES.

(DELIVERED).

	MARK.	HOGSHEAD. £ s. d.			BARREL. £ s. d.			KILDERKIN. £ s. d.			FIRKIN. s. d.	
East India Pale Ale	I.P.A.	4	1	0 -	2	14	0 -	1	7	0 -	13	6
Guinea Ale - - -	No. 6.	3	3	0 -	2	2	0 -	1	1	0 -	10	6
Light Bitter Ale -	B.A.	2	14	0 -	1	16	0 -	0	18	0 -	9	0
(Brewed expressly for Family use).												
Very Strong Ale -	XXXX.	4	10	0 -	3	0	0 -	1	10	0 -	15	0
Strong Ale - - -	BXXX.	4	1	0 -	2	14	0 -	1	7	0 -	13	6
Mild Dinner Ale -	No. 5.	3	12	0 -	2	8	0 -	1	4	0 -	12	0
Do. -	XX.	2	14	0 -	1	16	0 -	0	18	0 -	9	0
Do. -	X.	2	0	6 -	1	7	0 -	0	13	6 -	6	9
Table Beer - - -	T.	1	7	0 -	0	18	0 -	0	9	0 -	4	6
Double Brown Stout	D.B.S.	4	1	0 -	2	14	0 -	1	7	0 -	13	6
Double Stout - -	D.S.	3	12	0 -	2	8	0 -	1	4	0 -	12	0

BOTTLED ALES AND STOUTS.

These ALES AND STOUTS are brewed with water of first class brewing properties (analysis by E. R. SOUTHBY, ESQ., F.C.S.) and choice Malt and Hops, and are GUARANTEED PURE.

They are brilliant, sparkling, and particularly easy of digestion.

The **EAST INDIA PALE ALE** (I.P.A.) will bear comparison with the finest Burton Ales; and the LIGHT BITTER ALE (B.A.) which is brewed expressly for Family use, is a special ale, combining the advantages of the best German beers with a delicious flavour and aroma which cannot be surpassed.

FAT GOD'S BREWERY, Queen's Head, Iron Cross, near Evesham.
Alternatively known as the Queen's Head Brewery. Just inside Warwickshire but with an Evesham postal address, brewing began under Andrew Miller in the summer of 1997. Most of its production was consumed at the pub itself, but the free trade in the four surrounding counties was supplied. The brewery produced fourteen different beers, including Fat God's Bitter (ABV 3.6%), Fat God's Mild (4%) and Porter of the Vale (4.1%). The brewery closed in December 2001.

FLOWER & SONS LTD, Birmingham Road, Stratford-upon-Avon.
Founded in what was to become Brewery Street, Stratford, by Edward Fordham Flower in 1831. The company is listed in the 1835 directory as maltsters and brewers of One Elm. The family had formerly been brewers in Hertford from 1725. They emigrated to the USA in 1818 but Edward F. Flower returned to England in 1824. He established a brewery near Shaftesbury in Dorset but in 1830 moved to Stratford. He was joined by his son, Charles Flower, in 1852. By 1854 the company had acquired offices in Adelphi, London and St Ann's Square, Manchester. J. Hinks was appointed their Warwick and Stratford agent. By 1865 the company, then being run by sons Charles and Edgar Flower, acquired further stores in Beauchamp Square, Leamington. By 1866 sales stood at nearly £100,000. A new brewery was built along nearby Birmingham Road in 1870, with further extensions added in 1874 to a design by architect Joseph Lattimer. Its construction cost £35,000 but it allowed them to brew 4,000 barrels a week. In February 1877 the company registered its Shakespeare trademarks. The following year Henry Philip Gibbons was appointed manager of the company. The business

Above: *Flowers Brewery, Stratford-upon-Avon.*

Opposite: *Flowers post-war beer labels.*

registered as a limited liability company in February 1888. It developed an aggressive policy of taking over smaller breweries to acquire their tied houses. In 1896 profits for the year stood at £32,826. Turner's Caudlewell Brewery at Shipston-on-Stour was taken over earlier that same year. The Tavistock Brewery Co. of Tavistock, Devon, was taken over in 1899; Gardner Bros of Little Compton and Gillett's Swan Brewery of Moreton-in-Marsh in 1900; George Younger's Sunderland Brewery in 1922; Fortescue & Son of Bromsgrove in 1926; and Rowland's Brewery of Bewdley Street, Evesham, in 1948. By 1950 Flowers were producing 2,500 barrels a week and had a stable of 350 tied houses. Flowers themselves merged with J.W. Green Ltd of Luton, Bedfordshire, in 1954. Six of the nine new directors, though, were Luton men. Realising the good name that Flowers had acquired, Green's of Luton subsumed their name to become Flowers Breweries Ltd. The new company now controlled nearly 1,500 tied houses over twenty-two counties. Brewers Whitbread had acquired shares in a number of local breweries, including Davenport's of Birmingham and Flowers. In 1962 Sir Fordham Flower asked fellow director Colonel Whitbread to take over the running of Flowers, and the board gave its agreement to a merger. The firm was acquired by Whitbread & Co. Ltd, who merged it with West Country Breweries of Cheltenham to form Whitbread Flowers Ltd. In 1967 Whitbread decided to close the Stratford brewery and move all production to Cheltenham. Flowers Brewery closed in February 1968. The Luton brewery was also closed.

FRANKTON BAGBY BREWERY, The Old Stables, Church Lawford, Rugby.
This 5-barrel plant was opened in April 1999. Its beers include Squire's Brew (ABV 4.2%), Old Retainer (5%), First Born (4.2%), Midsummer Madness (3.8%) and Christmas Pudding (7%). The company supplies to some 150 free-trade outlets.

JAMES FREDERICK FRY, Rugby Brewery, Russell Street, Rugby.
Established in 1834. Fry was a brewer, maltster, corn and hop merchant. The office address is given as High Street in 1845, by which time the company was listed as 'brewers, porter dealer and cider merchants'. The brewery traded until 1868. The building has now been demolished.

GARDNER BROS, Little Compton.
Pre-1900. Taken over by Flowers of Stratford-upon-Avon in 1900.

GUY'S CLIFFE BREWERY, Coventry Road, Warwick.
Established by Seymour Archer in 1898 to supply the free trade. E.B. Preston was appointed manager in 1900, following Archer's death. Brewing was continued by the executors until sometime after 1906, whereafter the brewery finally closed.

HOME-BREWED (COVENTRY) LTD, Rock Brewery, Old Church Road, Foleshill, Coventry.
Established originally as Michael Spencer in the 1880s. Spencer was owner of the Royal Hotel and a dealer in yeast. Spencer's became a limited company in July 1896. The company later bought up licensed premises in Leicester Street, Upper Well Street and Cox Street, Coventry. A. Blair was appointed manager in 1903. The company re-registered in 1910 as Home-brewed (Coventry) Ltd, when taking over the business of Michael Spencer Ltd and its tied houses. The brewery was closed in 1913, after having been taken over by Thomas Pritchard. The building was later converted to R. White's mineral water plant.

GUY'S CLIFFE BREWERY Co.,
WARWICK.

Old-Fashioned

English Ales

and

Stouts . . .

From Pure MALT and HOPS.

TRIALS SOLICITED.

Special Terms to Free Houses.

NOTE ADDRESS—

GUY'S CLIFFE BREWERY
CO.,

M. SPENCER,
Brewer and Maltster,
FOLESHILL.

MILD & PALE ALES
Supplied in 36, 18, 9, & 4½ Gallon Casks.

JAGGARD & HIORNS, The Warwick Brewery, Wallace Street, Warwick.
The Warwick & Leamington Brewery Co. was established in February 1832 and moved into a converted factory and malthouse in Saltisford, which had been purchased for £4,000. Two of the original six partners, Richard Jaggard and Richard Hiorns, took control of the company as Hiorns, Jaggard & Co. Hiorns had formerly worked for London brewers Truman, Hanbury & Buxton. Hiorns died in 1845 and the company traded as Jaggard & Jaggard, being Richard and Joseph Jaggard. When Hiorn's son John joined the firm, it became Jaggard, Jaggard & Hiorns. With the death of Richard Jaggard and the retirement of Joseph, new partners William Thomas Jaggard and John Rose joined Hiorns. The new company of Hiorns, Jaggard & Rose found that they had inherited considerable debt due to the poor management of the former partners. In March 1864, with the company close to bankruptcy, the partners decided to put the company up for sale. It was purchased for £4,000 by Frank Speakman Webb and Percy Barron. The new company traded as Barron's (*see* Webb & Barron).

JOPE & JOPE, 47 Greyfriars Lane, Coventry.

Founded in 1864. The company were based at the Lion Brewery, Northampton. The Greyfriars site was a brewing subsidiary of that company. At Coventry they developed into spirit merchants. In 1867 the company became Coales, Allen & Cooper, while still retaining their Northampton links.

JUDGE'S, Church Lawford.

Established in May 1992 by Graham Judge. The company produced two beers, Barristers (ABV 3.5%) and Old Gavel Bender (5%). In the summer of 1995 the company moved to a 12-barrel plant in Constable Road, Hillmorton, Rugby. The brewery temporarily closed in April 1999 but reopened as Judge's Real Ale Brewery in June 1999. As the lease fell due on the struggling company, they relocated to Birmingham. As yet, the brewery has not resumed the production of beer. The Church End Brewery has now begun brewing Barristers Bitter and Old Gavel Bender.

LARDNER & SONS, Steam Brewery, Little Compton.

Founded in 1860. Although its address was given as Moreton-in-Marsh, the brewery was just inside the Warwickshire border. Listed as Henry Lardner in 1872, and Henry Lardner & Sons from 1879-92. The company was taken over by Hitchman & Co. of Chipping Norton in 1892. Brewing continued up to 1900.

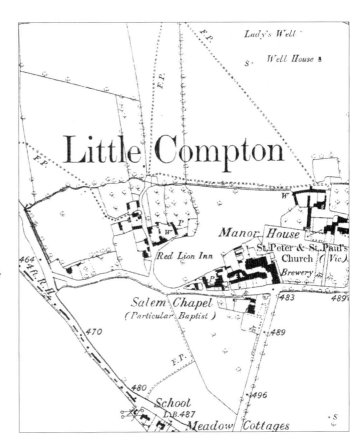

Opposite above: *Guy's Cliffe Brewery Co., Warwick.*

Opposite below: *An advertisement for Michael Spencer's Home-Brewed (Coventry) Ltd, 1892.*

Right: *A late nineteenth-century map showing Lardner's Brewery in Little Compton.*

JOHN LEWIS, Studley.
Beer retailer and brewer, 1854.

LEWIS, HADDON & ALLENBY, Leamington Brewery, Binswood, Leamington Spa.
Ale and porter brewers. Founded in 1839 by Stephen Lewis and Mr Sandeman, its brewery was
erected in 1840 by John Tone of Stoneleigh. In 1841 Sandeman was succeeded as Lewis' partner
by John Haddon. Allenby, Lewis' drapery business partner, also briefly joined the firm. With
expansion, John Payne was appointed their Black Country agent in 1844. Charles Dickins was
later appointed an agent in 1865. Following Lewis' death in 1871, the company briefly became
Lewis, Haddon & Co. of Kenilworth Road, Leamington. Soon after, the name was changed
again, when William Wells Ridley, who had joined the company in 1868, became a full partner.
In 1877 the company name changed to Lewis & Ridley. By 1879 the business had acquired
further premises at 20 Warwick Street, Rugby. The brewery was taken over by Lucas & Co. in
1885, along with its thirty-five tied houses, at a cost of £75,000 (*see* Lucas & Co. Ltd).

LITCHBOROUGH BREWERY, 140 Wood Street, Rugby.
Brewing from 1983. The business was taken over by Daventry brewers Liddington's. Brewing
ceased in 1986.

LUCAS & CO. LTD, 130 The Parade, Leamington Spa.
The company was founded by Stephen Lewis and Everitt Allenby in 1839. The brewery was built
to a design by London 'Brewers' Architect' Robert Davison. John Haddon became a partner in the
company in 1843. Upon Lewis' death in 1861, his two sons joined the company. One of the sons,
A.J. Lewis, took an active part in its running. W. Wells Ridley joined the company in 1865 and,
following the deaths of Everitt Allenby in 1871 and John Haddon in 1875, Lewis and Ridley
ran the business as the Leamington Brewery until 1885. That year the company and its 128
tied houses and off-licences were sold to the partnership of Morton Lucas, Percy Allan Leaf
and Gordon Lyon Bland. The new company traded as Lucas & Co. A new 60-quarter plant,
four storeys in height, was designed by London brewing architects Scamell & Colyer and built
by Wilson & Co., of Frome; it was installed in 1896. That same year, the company took over
Dutton & Hudson's Warwick Brewery in Swan Street, Warwick, along with its tied houses. The
firm registered as a limited company in July 1897 to acquire the business of Lucas & Co. along
with its eighty-eight freehold and thirty-six leasehold licensed houses. From 1914 the company's
general office was located at 4 Swan Street, Warwick. In 1928 the company took over the
business of Lucas, Blackwell & Arkwright of Leamington and Warwick Street, Rugby. They in
turn were taken over later that year, in November, by Ansell's, along with their 124 tied houses.
Brewing apparently continued up to the end of 1933, and the site was sold the following year.

LUCAS, BLACKWELL & ARKWRIGHT, The Brewery, Leamington, with offices
at 130 The Parade. Later, agencies were opened at 20 Warwick Street, Rugby and in Alcester,
Banbury, Leicester, Nottingham, London and Wolverhampton.
The company was established in 1887. By 1896 they were producing thirteen different brews,
including IPA, Light Sparkling Dinner Ale ('highly recommended', they advertised), a strong ale called
Stingo, four different Milds, a Brown Stout and a Porter. The IPA was sold at £3 the barrel, the Porter
at two guineas. At the outbreak of the First World War, the company had 124 tied houses. In 1928
Lucas, Blackwell & Arkwright were taken over by near namesakes Lucas & Co. of Leamington Spa.

THE ROYAL LEAMINGTON BREWERY.

LEWIS, HADDON, & ALLENBY,

Brewers of the Finest Ales and Porters,

LEAMINGTON, WARWICKSHIRE.

Sole Agents—BRIGHT & CO.,
11, Lower Castle-street, LIVERPOOL.

The Agents to the Royal Leamington Brewery being desirous of extending their business in this district for their celebrated Ales and Porters in Cask and Bottles, are better able to supply a fine pure extract of malt and hops and at a lower price than others. We beg to submit our prices as under :—

ALL FULL-SIZED BOTTLES.

	PER DOZEN.		
	Qrts.	Pts.	½-Pts.
East India Pale Ale, brilliant quality strongly recommended for invalids as an excellent tonic	5s. 3d.	3s. 4d.	2s. 2d.
Strong Mild Ale, XXX	5s. 3d.	3s. 4d.	2s. 2d.
A very pure Mild Ale, XX	4s. 9d.	2s. 6d.	2s. 0d.
A very agreeable light Ale for the dinner or supper	3s. 0d.	2s. 0d.	
Imperial Double Brown Stout	5s. 3d.	3s. 4d.	2s. 2d.
Double Brown Stout, very full and ripe	4s. 9d.	2s. 6d.	2s. 0d.
Brown Stout	4s. 0d.	2s. 3d.	1s. 9d.

Contracts with hotels and others for a regular supply of Ales and Porters in wood and bottle, in fine condition for immediate use. Bottles to be paid for on delivery, the same amount will be paid back when the bottles are returned.

Represented by Mr. JAMES SWINBURN,
BOTTLING STORES, LONDON STREET, corner of Derby-road,
SOUTHPORT

An early advertisement for Lewis, Haddon & Allenby's Leamington Brewery.

LEWIS & RIDLEY,

ALE AND **PORTER**

Brewers,

LEAMINGTON

THE LEAMINGTON BREWERY

·SPARKLING·

"GEM"

TRADE MARK

SHILLING ALE

WINE AND **SPIRIT**

Merchants,

1, Smithford Street,

COVENTRY.

FOR many years there has been a great and steadily increasing demand for a light, high-class Malt Liquor, which, while perfectly free from the headiness of ordinary Beers, shall at the same time possess the sparkling, pleasing, and nutritious qualities of a True Pale Ale.

MESSRS. LEWIS & RIDLEY, after a series of careful and varied experiments, are now enabled to announce that they have succeeded in producing an article which they believe will fully meet this requirement of the day.

The Water from which this Ale is brewed is drawn direct from the rock, and has been pronounced to be of "exceptional purity:"* the finest Malt and Hops are used in its production; whilst, by a peculiar process of fermentation, that sparkling effervescent character is given to the Ale, which forms so leading an element in the favourite beverages of the day.

The keeping properties of the "GEM" Ale will be found to be unrivalled, age simply serving to render its vinous qualities more marked and apparent.

The "GEM" Ale is supplied in Casks of 9, 18 and 36 Gallons, at the rate of One Shilling per Gallon, subject to the usual Cash Discount, a price only equal therefore to that of an ordinary Family Dinner Ale.

A Label, bearing the Trade Mark as above, is affixed to each cask, without which none are genuine.

* Analysis by E. R. SOUTHBY, Esq., M.R.C.S., the eminent Consulting Chemist.

LIST OF PRICES.

BRAND.		BAR.	KIL.	FIR.	BRAND.		BAR.	KIL.	FIR.
EIPA	East India Pale Ale	60/	30/		BA	Bitter Ale	36/	18/	9/
IPA	India Pale Ale . .	54/	27/	13/6	X	Mild Ale	30/	15/	7/6
LS	Strong Ale . . .	66/	33/		TS	Treble Stout . . .	60/	30/	
XXXX	Strong Ale . . .	60/	30/			Brewed specially for invalids			
XXXK	Mild Ale . . .	54/	27/		DBS	Double Brown Stout	54/	27/	13/6
XXX	Mild Ale	48/	24/	12/	BS	Brown Stout . . .	48/	24/	12/
XXK	Mild Ale . . .	42/	21/	10/6	P	Porter	42/	21/	10/6

"GEM" SPARKLING DINNER ALE (*Highly Recommended*).

A Discount of 5 per Cent. allowed for Cash within 1 Month from date of Invoice.

An 1880 advertisement for Lewis & Ridley and a price list of beers.

	WILLIAM WELLS RIDLEY, on behalf of Self and Partner, ARTHUR JAMES LEWIS, trading as LEWIS AND RIDLEY, Leamington, Warwickshire; Brewers.	43	Beer.	21,602	7th Aug. 1880.

ALES   STOUTS   WINES   SPIRITS

LUCAS & Co. Ltd.

TRADE   MARK

Visitors

REQUIRING LIQUID REFRESHMENTS WILL FIND THEM DELIGHTFULLY SERVED IN THE PLEASANTEST LOUNGE IN THE TOWN, at

130, PARADE

(OPPOSITE TOWN HALL)

The **BREWERY**, Leamington Spa

Branch 130, PARADE, LEAMINGTON   Telephone:
Offices: 4, SWAN STREET, WARWICK   19 LEAMINGTON

Top: *Lewis & Ridley's registered trademark, 1880.*

Above: *An advertisement for Lucas & Co.*

Right: *Lucas & Co.'s Leamington Brewery, 1897.*

THE LEAMINGTON BREWERY.

LUCAS, BLACKWELL & ARKWRIGHT,

PALE ALE,
STOUT AND PORTER BREWERS.

BREWERS AND WINE AND SPIRIT MERCHANTS.
THE BREWERY, & 130, THE PARADE, LEAMINGTON.

REGISTERED

Mild and Pale brewed with the Hops, and their strength,

TRADE  MARK.

Ales and Stouts Finest Malt and celebrated for flavour & brilliancy.

BRAND ON CASK.	LIST OF PRICES.								BAR.	KIL.	FIR.
EIPA	EAST INDIA PAL...	...	...	...	...	...	...	...	60s.	30s.	15s.
IPA	INDIA PALE ALE	...	...	...	...	...	...	...	54s.	27s.	13s. 6d.
PA	PALE ALE	...	...	...	...	...	...	...	42s.	21s.	10s. 6d.
'GEM'	LIGHT SPARKLING DINNER ALE (highly recommended)					...	...	36s.	18s.	9s.
'STINGO'	STRONG ALE...	...	...	...	...	...	...	...	72s.	36s.	18s.
XXXX	STRONG ALE...	...	...	...	...	...	...	...	60s.	30s.	15s.
XXXK	MILD ALE	...	...	...	...	...	...	...	54s.	27s.	13s. 6d.
XXX	MILD ALE	...	...	...	...	...	...	...	48s.	24s.	12s.
XX	MILD ALE	...	...	...	...	...	...	...	36s.	18s.	9s.
X	MILD ALE	...	...	...	...	...	...	...	30s.	15s.	7s. 6d.
DBS	DOUBLE BROWN STOUT	...	...	...	...	...	...	...	54s.	27s.	13s. 6d.
BS	BROWN STOUT	...	...	...	...	...	...	...	48s.	24s.	12s.
P	PORTER	...	...	...	...	...	...	...	42s.	21s.	10s. 6d.

LIST OF AGENCIES.

RUGBY—20, Warwick Street.
ALCESTER & REDDITCH—Bear Hotel, Alcester.
BANBURY—55, High Street.
WARWICK—Old Square.
STRATFORD-ON-AVON—40, Greenhill St.
LEICESTER—41, Market Place.
HORSHAM—H. Churchman, West St.
WELLINGBOROUGH—1, Silver Street.

NOTTINGHAM — Samuel Parr, South Sherwood Street.
RUSHDEN—W. W. Smith, Leamington House.
NORTHAMPTON — Simpson & Son, 9, Sheep Street.
WELSHPOOL—Saml.Morris,CornerShop.
IRTHLINGBORO'—F.A. Parsons,High St.
COWFOLD—W. Spinks.

LONDON—111, Gloucester Road and 32, Sussex Place, South Kensington.
LONG SUTTON—Fletcher & Son.
ASHBY DE LA ZOUCH—E. Simpkin, Market Place.
KEIGHLEY—C. Stanley, 23 Low Street.
WOLVERHAMPTON—Thos. Jones, Gosebrook Wharf,StaffordRd.,Bushbury
ATHERSTONE—W. H. Allcock, Long St.

Orders received at the Brewery, or at the Branch Office, 130, The Parade (which is connected with the Head Office by telephone), or at any of the above Agencies.

Telegrams—"BREWERY," LEAMINGTON.   Telephone No. 519.

Lucas, Blackwell & Arkwright's Leamington Brewery price list, 1896.

WILLIAM JOHN LYNCH, White Friar Model Brewery, 73 Much Park Street and White Friar Lane, Coventry.
Established in 1911, this small brewery was in existence up to 1935. It had at least two tied houses.

JAMES MARRIOTT & SON, Midland Brewery, 127 Much Park Street, Coventry.
Established in 1868. Marriott had formerly been head brewer at Jaggard & Hiorns Warwick Brewery. In 1877 the firm became Phillips & Marriott Ltd, when James Marriott retired (*see* Phillips & Marriott).

EDWARD MOXON, Trent Valley Brewery Co., Easenhall.
Brewers and maltsters. Founded by 1865, the company had become William, Thomas Dand and John Moxon by 1868. *White's History, Gazeteer & Directory* for 1874 describes the brewery as 'large'. In that year, George Fern appears as manager. Previously, in 1871, the company had established stores at Brinklow, with further stores at Stretton-under-Fosse and Rugby by 1878. Thomas Dand Moxon is also listed separately as a brewer at Easenhall from 1868-72. The business was being run by Thomas Moxon in 1900. Edward Moxon joined him in 1908, taking over the running of the brewery in 1913. The company were advertised as brewers during the 1930s but had ceased brewing by 1940, possibly due to wartime shortages.

NORTH COTSWOLD BREWERY, near Shipston-on-Stour.
Just within the Warwickshire border, although the postal address is given as Moreton-in-Marsh, Gloucestershire. Opened by David and Roger Tilbrook in the spring of 1999, it has a 10-barrel plant supplying forty outlets, including the former home-brew house Black Horse Inn at Shipston-on-Stour. The brewery produces Genesis (ABV 4%), Four Shires (4.2%) and a seasonal beer, Solstice (3.7%).

NUNEATON BREWERY CO. LTD, Bridge Street, Nuneaton.
The brewery was founded by John Knowles, a former miller, and brewing began on 16 October 1878. Water was drawn from a well dug to a depth of 223ft. The brewery plant was purchased from Hoxley's of Frome and C. Greenhill was appointed manager. In May of the following year, extensions were added to the brewery. By May 1881, the brewery was in financial straits and was put up for sale by auction. Failing to meet its reserve, it was withdrawn but in November it was purchased by private treaty. Its new owner was Griff Alkin, a quarry owner of Hartshill. Alkin's brewing venture was not a success and in May 1882 the brewery was again put up for auction. The sales particulars relate that the brewery was a 10-quarter steam brewery, with a brewery tap attached. Its new buyer was Adams Holdford Adams. By February 1883 they were brewing nine different beers, including mild, bitter, stout and porter. In 1884 the business became Adams, Holdford & Co. In 1889, though, the business failed and was bought up by the executors of Samuel Wright, of the Victoria Brewery, Walkern, Hertfordshire. The building was put up for auction on 30 January 1890. Again it failed to make its reserve and was withdrawn. Subsequently the building was demolished and the site was sold off.

JOSEPH OWEN Common brewer, 1806 (*see* Summerfield, Lloyd & Owen).

THOMAS PARIS, Public Brewery, Clemens Street, Leamington Spa, 1817.
There is an entry for the brewery in W. Field's *New Guide to Warwick & Leamington* for 1817. It is possible that this brewery may have evolved into Lewis, Haddon & Allenby's Leamington Brewery.

PUBLIC ACCOMMODATIONS.

Hotels and Boarding Houses.

The Royal Hotel and Boarding House, High-Street, Mr. M. COPPS.
Bedford Hotel & Boarding House, Union-Parade, Mr. J. WILLIAMS.
Bath Hotel and Boarding House, Bath-Street, Mrs. SMITH.
Blenheim Hotel & Boarding House, Clemens-St. Mr. RACKSTROW.

Public Coffee Room,

At Copps' Royal Hotel and Boarding-House.

Inns.

Crown Inn, High-Street, ... Mr. STANLEY.
Bowling Green Inn, ... Mrs. SHAW.

Ordinaries.

At the BATH HOTEL, every Day, at Three o'Clock.—Sundays at Four.
At the CROWN INN, every Day, at Three.

Public Houses.

Angel, Cross Street, New-Town.	Half Moon, Satchwell-Street,
Golden Lion, Do.	Red Lion—White Swan.

** Porters may be had at any of the Inns.

Public Brewery.

Mr. T. PARIS, (the Proprietor,) Clemens-Street.

Porter Vaults,

Under the Assembly Rooms, Union-Parade.
London Porter from the Brewery of Felix Calvert and Co. is constantly
on Sale here, by C. BYRN.

** Orders received at No. 18, Union Parade Cottage.

London and Country Porter, sold also by J. BROOMHALL, at his
Vaults, under Perry's Museum, Clemens'-Street.

Livery Stables, &c.

BEDFORD (late King's) MEWS, opposite the Bedford Hotel.
MERRY'S (late Probett's) Hunting & Livery Stables, Clemens'-Street.
STANLEY'S Livery Stables, High-Street.
Lock-up Coach-Houses and Stabling, at COPPS'S Royal Hotel.
Stabling to the Bath Hotel.

Thomas Paris' Brewery in Clemens Street, from an 1817 guide to Warwick and Leamington.

DANIEL PETTIFOR & SONS, Steam Brewery, Ansty.
The company, along with its twenty tied houses, was acquired by Marston, Thompson & Evershed of Burton-on-Trent in 1900. Curiously there are no entries for this brewery in any *Kelly's Directory* prior to this.

JOSEPH PHILLIPS & SON, Coventry Brewery, Leicester Row, Coventry.
Phillips took over the old brewery business of Summerfield, Lloyd & Owen in 1827. In 1834 Joseph's son, Henry, took over the running of the business. He is listed in the *Post Office Directory* of 1845 as an ale and porter brewer. In 1849 the brewery was taken over by William Ratcliff (*see* William Ratcliff).

PHILLIPS & MARRIOTT, Midland Brewery, 127 Much Park Street, Coventry.
Established in 1877, being the former brewery of James Marriott & Son. Following its takeover, Frank Phillips took control of the new company. In 1896 the brewery had only three tied houses, at Earl Street, Spon Street and Little Park Street. Following the construction of a new 80-quarter malting house in Much Park Street, costing £7,000, the company began acquiring tied houses. In January 1900 they became a limited liability company in order to acquire the business of the late William Ratcliff, of the Coventry Brewery in Leicester Road, Coventry. By this merger, their tied houses rose to sixty-three. Frank Phillips died in February 1901. In December of that year the company, facing a fall-off in profits, agreed at their annual general meeting to write off losses of £9,678, which it seemed unlikely that they would ever recover. The company went into decline. Previously, in September 1901, they had been prosecuted for defrauding the Inland Revenue by adulterating their beer by adding glucose. In 1904 the company attempted to buy themselves out of their decline and opened additional premises at Albert Street, Rugby and Long Street, Atherstone. In 1909 a new 30-quarter brewery was erected to a design by Messrs William Bradford & Sons, Architects and Brewers' Consulting Engineers of Regent Street, London. The company was turned around and returned, for a time, to the black. Following the end of the First World War, the brewery – not in isolation it should be added – went into decline. They found it difficult to compete. In 1922 the company's trading profits were as low as £4,265. A number of their tied houses were leasehold and as the leases fell, other bigger breweries bought them up, thus denying them these vital outlets. Phillips & Marriott was taken over by Bass, Ratcliff & Gretton of Burton-on-Trent in 1924, along with their tied houses. Brewing was terminated at the site. The old brewery was eventually demolished in 1971.

PHIPPS PICKERING & CO. LTD, St Nicholas Street, Coventry.
Founded in 1883. The company became Phipps & Co. in 1890. Arthur William Massey was appointed manager. By 1896 the company had established premises at Sheep Street, Stratford-upon-Avon, and in 1900 further premises were acquired at Longford, Coventry. Isaac Courts was appointed manager in 1903. He was succeeded by I. Sephton in 1920. The brewery ceased production by 1924.

WILLIAM RATCLIFF, The Coventry Brewery, 10 Leicester Row, Coventry.
Established in 1849, taking over the former premises of Joseph Phillips & Son. Ratcliff styled the Coventry brewery as the 'oldest established brewery in the Midlands'. This claim does not, however, stand up to scrutiny as Bass of Burton-on-Trent was founded in 1777. Samuel Swinbourn of Sutton Coldfield was appointed an agent of the company in 1871. Ratcliff had died by 1899 and his executors continued running the business up to 1900, whereafter it was

Phillips & Marriott's new brewery in Coventry, 1909.

taken over by Phillips & Marriott Ltd of Much Park Street. The brewery buildings were sold to Coventry Corporation in 1912. They became a council depot. The old brewery was demolished and the site has since been redeveloped.

SHIPSTON BREWERY, Stratford Road, Shipston-on-Stour.
Established by 1890. The company opened up further stores at Greenhill Street, Stratford-upon-Avon. Additional premises were acquired at Arden Street, Stratford by 1896. The brewery closed down before the First World War.

SIMMONDS & CO., The Brewery, Bear & Bacculus, High Street, near Lord Leycester's Hospital, West Gate, Warwick.
Listed during the late nineteenth century as common brewers, they supplied their own house and the free trade. The pub is now a private house.

SLAUGHTERHOUSE BREWERY, Emscote Road, Warwick.
Brewer Chris Willsmore established this 4-barrel plant brewery in an old slaughterhouse in April 2003. The plant came from the original Church End Brewery at Shustoke, following its move to Nuneaton. Beers include Swillmore Bitter (ABV 4.6%), Swillmore Pale Ale (ABV 4.5%) and a winter ale, Wild Boar (5.2%).

JOHN SODEN, Spon Street Brewery, Coventry.
Established by auctioneer and brewer John Soden pre-1845, behind the Eagle public house at 48 Spon Street. Previously Soden had been landlord and brewer at the Half Moon in Earl Street. He had become a maltster, brewer and wine and spirit merchant by 1854. Apparently dead by 1860, his widow continued the business for a further year.

MICHAEL SPENCER, Rock Brewery, Foleshill, Coventry.
See Home-brewed (Coventry) Ltd.

STEWARD & HEAD, Stratford-upon-Avon.
Common brewers, taken over by Charrington's in 1833, subsequently trading as Charrington & Head. Production was later moved to Burton-on-Trent.

STUDLEY BREWERY, Old Washford Mill, Icknield Street, Studley.
A short-lived home-brew house serving the Seven Wonder Inn Group and also the free trade. 'Real Ale brewed to an original recipe of 1741' was how it advertised itself. The company was founded at a former needle-making factory in September 1978 by Michael Cannon. The brewery was situated in an outbuilding behind the mill, which had been converted into a public house-cum-restaurant. They brewed three beers: Old Glory, Studley Bitter and Studley Giant. At capacity they were brewing 1,000 gallons a week. Complications set in, with recurring problems concerning wild yeast infection. This affected the quality of the beer, which became quite variable. Brewing ceased in October 1982 and the pub bought in beer, notably from the Black Country brewers Holden's of Woodsetton.

STUDLEY BREWERY CO., Studley.
Originated by John Thompson in 1880. Richard Thomas Scholefield was listed as manager in 1888 (*see* Thompson's Brewery Ltd).

SUMMERFIELD, LLOYD & CO., Coventry

Brewery, Leicester Row, Coventry.

Partners William Summerfield and David Lloyd, of the Birmingham banking family, founded the company in 1801. It is first listed in *Holden's Triennial Directory* for 1805-07. By 1808 the company had become the Coventry Porter Brewery of Summerfield, Lloyd & Owen. In 1824 the business was taken over by Joseph Phillips & Son.

THOMPSON'S BREWERY LTD, Bell

Brewery, High Street, Studley.

Registered as a company by John Thompson in 1892 to acquire the Studley Brewery Co. The brewery was situated alongside and behind the Bell Inn. At its height, it was producing between 65 and 100 barrels of Bell Ales a week. In 1928 Thompson's son took over the running of the business. By then, production had been reduced to around 30 barrels but the company was also bottling and distributing Guinness at their plant. In addition to its tied houses, the brewery also supplied the local free trade, including Astwood and Studley cricket clubs. The brewery and its five tied houses were bought up by M&B in 1945. The brewery was demolished in 1962. The site has since been converted into a beer garden.

Above: *A bottle label from Thompson's Brewery.*

Below: *Simple Simon, Emscote Road, Warwick. An outlet for the Slaughterhouse Brewery.*

Opposite above: *Thompson's Bell Brewery, Studley, c. 1910.*

Opposite below: *The Throckmorton Arms, Coughton, 1934. A Thompson's house.*

H.E. THORNLEY LTD, Radford Hall Brewery, Radford Semele, Leamington Spa. Town office at 146 The Parade, Leamington Spa. Founded in 1899. The company merged with Benjamin Kelsey Ltd of Birmingham in 1933 to form Thornley Kelsey Ltd. The company was later renamed Benjamin Kelsey Ltd. Radford Hall Brewery closed in October 1968, whereafter the company concentrated on its wholesale wine business. Their sixty-eight tied houses were sold off, the majority being bought by Davenport's of Birmingham. The brewery was later demolished.

TRENT VALLEY BREWERY
(*See* Edward Moxon.)

WILLIAM TURNER, Caudlewell Brewery, Shipston-on-Stour.
Now in Warwickshire but then in a detached section of Worcestershire, the brewery was founded in 1882. It first appears in *Kelly's Directory* for 1884. The Caudlewell Brewery was situated along Stratford Road, just north-east of the town. By 1894 the company had diversified into the spirits trade. The brewery was taken over by Flowers of Stratford in 1896.

Above: *The White Lion, Radford Semele. A Thornley's house.*

Opposite: *Thornley's beer bottle lables*

WALSH'S BAKEHOUSE BREWERY, Scar Bank Warwick.
The brewery was established in the Walsh family bakery in June 2003. It has a 5-barrel plant, acquired from the old Flyer & Firkin in Reading. At present the company brew three regular beers: Bakehouse Bitter (ABV 3.8%), Flying Top (4.4%) and a premium ale, Old Gridlap (5.0%). Nine seasonal ales are promised. In February 2004, the brewery had three regular and ten occasional outlets.

WARWICKSHIRE BEER CO., Old Village Bakery, Queen's Street, Cubbington, near Leamington Spa.
Established by Philip Page, formerly of the Warwickshire Brewery Ltd, in November 1998. In May 2001 the company purchased the Market Tavern as its principal outlet. The brewery began by producing six barrels a week, expanding to some twenty-six by 2000, supplying eighty outlets. Its range includes First Gold (ABV 4.9%), Cascade (4.6%), Best Bitter (3.9%), Kingmaker (5.5%), Falstaff (4.4%) and Lady Godiva (4.2%). The brewery also sells bottled beer and 10-litre polypins.

WARWICK BREWERY CO., The Brewery, Wallace Street, Warwick.
Webb & Barron, proprietors, 1867-72. Percy Barron & Co., 1874-78.

An interior view of Walsh's Bakehouse Brewery, Warwick.

WARWICKSHIRE BREWERY LTD, Princes Drive, Kenilworth.

Established in December 1995 by Philip Page. It closed in late September 1997.

WEBB & BARRON, Warwick Brewery, Swan Street, Warwick.

The partnership of Frank Speakman Webb and Percy Barron, who bought up the Warwick Brewery, then in liquidation, from Hiorns, Jaggard & Rose in 1864, for £4,250. The business traded under Barron's name until 1879, when it was taken over by Jonas Paston of Dutton & Sons of Witney, Oxfordshire, for £16,500. At the time the brewery was producing 9,050 barrels a year, and had twelve tied houses (*see* Dutton & Hudson).

WINNALL & GARRETT, Britannia Brewery, Shipston-on-Stour, with further premises at Waterside, Stratford-upon-Avon.

William George Shaw is listed as their agent for 1878. In 1879 the company became Winnall, Garrett & Smith, having moved to Canal Wharf, Stratford, and with further premises at 19 Jury Street, Warwick. Brewing ceased and the company acted as bottlers for other breweries for a time.

WIZARD BREWERY, Whichford, Shipston-on-Stour.

A 1¼-barrel plant established by Michael Garner in March 2003. Plans were for the nearby Norman Knight public house to take most of the production at first, then to expand to the free trade. Beers include One for the Toad (ABV 3.6%), One for Yourself (4.0%) and Mother in Law (4.0%).

EDWARD WOODFIELD, Regent Brewery, behind the Birmingham Tavern, Wise Street, Leamington Spa.

Founded by William Fowler pre-1814, it had been taken over by Edward Woodfield by 1828. Henry Woodfield had succeeded his father by 1834. The brewery appears to have been supplying beer to a number of other outlets in addition to its own public house tap. The Regent Brewery was closed by 1845.

BIBLIOGRAPHY

Brewers' Journal, 1870-1930.

Corran, Henry Stanley, *A History of Brewing*, David & Charles, 1975.

Directories of Warwickshire, 1785-1940.

Good Beer Guide, CAMRA, 1974-2003.

Luckett, Fred, Ken Flint and Peter Lee, *A History of Brewing in Warwickshire*, CAMRA, 1983.

Manual of British & Foreign Brewery Companies, 1899-1965.

Matthias, Peter, *The Brewing Industry in England, 1730-1830*, CUP, 1959.

Parliamentary Papers, 1890-91, (c.28) LXXXVIII.

Richmond, Lesley and Alison Turton, *The Brewing Industry – A Guide to Historical Records*, MUP, 1990.

INDEX

Please note that retail brewers have not been indexed as they are listed in alphabetical order by town or village within the text.

Other local titles published by Tempus

Stratford-upon-Avon and Beyond

JOHN D. OLDFIELD

In this sparkling collection of over 200 old photographs and postcards, Stratford and the villages of three counties from the surrounding area are explored. From images of the streets and buildings, pubs and hotels, to the beauty of the river and surrounding countryside, and the development of the major insurance company and largest employer in the area – the NFU Mutual – all aspects of working and social life are chronicled here.

0 7524 0685 X

Haunted Coventry

DAVID McGRORY

When Coventry sleeps, the dead wander the streets! Or so it is said in Haunted Coventry, which features spooky stories from the city and surrounding area. Within these pages you will find the Phantom Monk of St Mary's Hall, ghostly grey ladies, a spectre which appears to do the washing up and the Devil himself, rattling chains at Whitefriars.

0 7524 3708 9

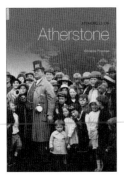

Memories of Atherstone

CHRISTINE FREEMAN

This book brings together the personal memories of people who have lived and worked in Atherstone, vividly recalling childhood and schooldays, shops and working life, leisure and entertainment, and the war years. It is the people, whose experiences and reminiscences are recorded here, who have shaped the area into the fascinating place it is today. The many absorbing stories are complemented by over 100 photographs from the participants' private collections.

0 7524 3422 5

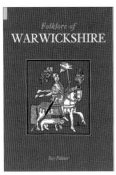

Folklore of Warwickshire

ROY PALMER

Warwickshire is a county steeped in tradition, folklore and mythology. This new illustrated edition is a fascinating study of folklore rooted firmly within the context of popular culture and history. There are tales of saints and sinners, sports and pastimes, fairs and wakes, folk song and balladry, as well as the passage rites of marriage, birth and death.

0 7524 3359 8

If you are interested in purchasing other books published by Tempus, or in case you have difficulty finding any Tempus books in your local bookshop, you can also place orders directly through our website

www.tempus-publishing.com